IN CHRIST JESUS

IN CHRIST JESUS

THE SPHERE OF THE BELIEVER'S LIFE

BY

ARTHUR T. PIERSON

CURIOSMITH

MINNEAPOLIS

2012

Published by Curiosmith.
P. O. Box 390293, Minneapolis, Minnesota, 55439, USA.
Internet: curiosmith.com.
E-mail: shopkeeper@curiosmith.com.

Previously published T. C. HORTON, who bought the copyright from
Funk & Wagnalls Company, 1898.

ISBN 9781935626626

CONTENTS

DEDICATION . . . 7

FOREWORD . . . 9

INTRODUCTION . . . 9

CHAPTER 1 — THE EPISTLE TO THE ROMANS . . . 15

CHAPTER 2 — THE EPISTLES TO THE CORINTHIANS . . . 29

CHAPTER 3 — THE EPISTLE TO THE GALATIANS . . . 39

CHAPTER 4 — THE EPISTLE TO THE EPHESIANS . . . 53

CHAPTER 5 — THE EPISTLE TO THE PHILIPPIANS . . . 65

CHAPTER 6 — THE EPISTLE TO THE COLOSSIANS . . . 77

CHAPTER 7 — THE EPISTLES TO THE THESSALONIANS . . . 87

CHAPTER 8 — CONCLUSION . . . 97

To my brother, beloved
In Christ Jesus,
𝕽𝖊𝖛. 𝕮. 𝕴. 𝕾𝖈𝖔𝖋𝖎𝖊𝖑𝖉. 𝕯. 𝕯.,
whose fellowship in faith
and Bible study
have done much to stimulate and
encourage Christian believers;
and to all who
have found in Christ Jesus
the Sphere
of all Life and Blessing,
this book is inscribed.

INTRODUCTION

There is in a Russian palace, a famous "Saloon of Beauty," wherein are hung over eight hundred and fifty portraits of young maidens. These pictures were painted by Count Rotari, for Catharine the Second, the Russian empress; and the artist made a journey, through the fifty provinces of that vast empire of the north, to find his models.

In these superb portraits that cover the walls of this saloon, there is said to be a curiously expressed compliment to the artist's royal patron, a compliment half concealed and half revealed. In each separate picture, it is said, might be detected, by the close observer, some hidden, delicate reference to the empress for whom they were painted. Here a feature of Catharine appears; there an attitude is reproduced, some act, some favorite adornment or environment, some jewel, fashion, flower, style of dress, or manner of life—something peculiar to, or characteristic of, the empress—so that the walls of the saloon are lined with just so many silent tributes to her beauty, or compliments to her taste. So inventive and ingenious is the spirit of human flattery when it seeks to glorify a human fellow-mortal, breaking its flask of lavish praise on the feet of an earthly monarch.

The Word of God is a picture-gallery, and it is adorned with tributes to the blessed Christ of God, the Savior of mankind. Here a prophetic portrait of the coming One, and there an historic portrayal of Him who has come, here a typical sacrifice, and there the bleeding Lamb to whom all sacrifice looked forward; here a person or an event that foreshadowed the greatest of persons and the events that are the turning-points of history; now a parable, a poem, an object-lesson, and then a simple narration or exposition or explanation, that fills with divine meaning the mysteries that have hid their meaning for ages, waiting for the key that should unlock them. But, in whatever form or fashion, whatever guise of fact or fancy, prophecy or history, parable or miracle, type or antitype, allegory or narrative, a discerning eye may everywhere find HIM—God's appointed Messiah, God's anointed Christ. Not a human grace that has not been a faint forecast or reflection of His beauty, in whom all grace was enshrined and enthroned—not a virtue that is not a new exhibition of His attractiveness. All that is glorious is but a phase of His infinite excellence, and so all truth and holiness, found in the Holy Scripture, are only a new tribute to Him who is the Truth, the Holy One of God.

This language is no exaggeration; on such a theme not only is exaggeration impossible, but the utmost superlative of human language falls infinitely short of His divine worth, before whose indescribable glory cherubim and seraphim can only bow, veiling their faces and covering their feet. The nearer we come to the very throne where such majesty sits, the more are we awed into silence. The more we know of Him, the less we seem to know, for the more boundless and limitless appears what remains to be known. Nothing is so conspicuous a seal of God upon the written Word, as the fact that everywhere, from Genesis to Revelation, we may find the Christ; and nothing more sets the seal of God upon the living Word than the fact that He alone explains and reveals the Scriptures.

Our present undertaking is a very simple one. We seek to show, by a few examples, the boundless range and scope of one brief phrase of two or three short words: IN CHRIST, or, IN CHRIST JESUS. A very small key may open a very complex lock and a very large door, and that door may itself lead into a vast building with priceless stores of wealth and beauty. This brief phrase—a preposition followed by a proper name—is the key to the whole New Testament.

Those three short words, *"in Christ Jesus,"* are, without doubt, the most important ever written, even by an inspired pen, to express the mutual relation of the believer and Christ. They occur, with their equivalents, over one hundred and thirty times. Sometimes we meet the expression, *in Christ*, or *in Christ Jesus*, and again *in Him*, or *in Whom,* etc. And sometimes this sacred name, or its equivalent pronoun, is found associated with other prepositions—*through, with, by;* but the thought is essentially the same. Such repetition and variety must have some intense meaning. When, in the Word of God, a phrase like this occurs so often, and with such manifold applications, it can not be a matter of accident; there is a deep design. God's Spirit is bringing a truth of the highest importance before us, repeating for the sake of emphasis, compelling even the careless reader to give heed as to some vital teaching.

What that teaching is, in this case, it is our present purpose to inquire, and, in the light of the Scripture itself, to answer.

First of all, we should carefully settle what this phrase, in Christ, or in Christ Jesus, means.

If there be one truth of the Gospel that is fundamental, and underlies all else, it is this: *A new life in Christ Jesus*. He, Himself, clearly and forcibly expressed it in John 15:4: "Abide in

Me and I in you." By a matchless parable our Lord there taught us that all believers are branches of the Living Vine, and that, apart from Him, we are nothing and can do nothing, because we have in us no *life*. This truth finds expression in many ways in the Holy Scripture, but most frequently in that short and simple phrase we are now considering—in Christ Jesus.

Such a phrase suggests that He is to the believer THE SPHERE OF THIS NEW LIFE OR BEING. Let us observe—a *sphere* rather than a *circle*. A circle surrounds us, but only *on one plane;* but a sphere encompasses, envelopes us, surrounding us in every direction and on every plane. If you draw a circle on the floor, and step within its circumference, you are within it only on the level of the floor. But, if that circle could become a sphere, and you be within it, it would on every side surround you—above and below, before and behind, on the right hand and on the left. Moreover, the sphere that *surrounds* you also *separates* you from whatever is outside of it. Again, in proportion as such a sphere is strong it also *protects* whatever is within it from all that is without—from all external foes or perils. And yet again, it *supplies*, to whomsoever is within it, whatever it contains. This may help us to understand the great truth taught with such clearness, especially in the New Testament. Christ is there presented throughout as the sphere of the believer's whole life and being, and in this truth are included these conditions:

First, Christ Jesus surrounds or embraces the believer, in His own life; second, He separates the believer in Himself from all hostile influences; third, He protects him in Himself from all perils and foes of his life; fourth, He provides and supplies in Himself all that is needful.

We shall see a further evidence of the vital importance of the phrase, in Christ, in the fact that these two words unlock and interpret every separate book in the New Testament. Here is

God's own key, whereby we may open all the various doors and enter all the glorious rooms in this Palace Beautiful, and explore all the apartments in the house of the heavenly Interpreter, from Matthew to the Apocalypse, where the door is opened into heaven. Each of the four Gospel narratives, the book of the Acts, all of the Epistles of Paul and Peter, James and John, and Jude, with the mysterious Revelation of Jesus Christ, show us some new relation sustained by Christ Jesus to the believer, some new aspect of Christ as his sphere of being, some new benefit or blessing enjoyed by him who is thus in Christ Jesus.

To demonstrate and illustrate this is the aim of this study of the New Testament. And, for brevity's sake, it may be well to confine our examination to the *Epistles of Paul,* from Romans to Thessalonians, which will be seen to bear to each other, and to the phrase we are studying, a unique and complete relation. We shall trace this phrase in every one of these epistles, and find it sometimes recurring with marked frequency and variety, generally very close to the very beginning of each epistle; and usually we shall find also that the first occurrence of the phrase, in each epistle, determines its particular relation to that particular book, thus giving us a key to the special phase of the general subject presented in that epistle. The more we study the phrase and the various instances and peculiar varieties of such recurrence, the more shall we be convinced of its vital importance to all practical holy living.

In tracing the uses and bearings of this significant phrase, it will serve the purpose we have in view to regard the epistles to each of the various churches as *one,* even when there are two. This will give us *seven instances* of the application of the phrase, which will be found to be similar in the two Epistles to the Corinthians and the two addressed to the Thessalonians. We may for our purpose, therefore, regard both epistles in each of these cases as parts of one; and we shall, therefore, have before us this simple study: to examine the particular application of this expression, in Christ, or in Christ Jesus, as used by Paul in writing to the Romans, the Corinthians, the Galatians, the Ephesians, the Philippians, the Colossians, and the Thessalonians.

CHAPTER 1

THE EPISTLE TO THE ROMANS

At the very opening of this letter (1:5), we read these words: "By whom," or "through whom," we have received grace, etc., *i.e.*, through God's Son, Jesus Christ, our Lord; and, in chapter 3:24, "Being *justified* freely by His grace through the *Redemption* that is *in Christ Jesus."* Here then we have the key to the Epistle to the Romans: *Grace, Justification, Redemption, in and through Christ Jesus;* or, to put it briefly, *Justified in Christ.*

This is manifestly the first step, for this conception belongs first in order. We can have, in Christ Jesus, nothing else, unless and until we have first justification—*a new standing before God.*

Paul is inspired to begin this epistle by showing that all men, Jews and Gentiles alike, are included under sin and therefore involved in condemnation. No sinner has before him any prospect but divine wrath, until he is first freed from the law, no longer under condemnation. Hence the first unfolding of grace in the Epistles is the plain revelation of God's marvelous plan, whereby sinners get the standing of saints. The question, how the condemned may become justified; the lost, saved; the alienated, reconciled; this is the question first and fully answered in this epistle.

If we examine chapter 5:1-11, we shall eight times meet the phrase, through, by, or in Jesus Christ; or its equivalent. And here are represented, as bestowed upon us freely, in or through Him, justification, peace with God, access by faith, a gracious standing, rejoicing in hope of the glory of God; and, even in the experience of tribulation, the love of God shed abroad in the heart, salvation from wrath, reconciliation, safekeeping in His life, perpetual joy in God, etc.[1]

Blessed indeed to meet, as we begin our study of the epistles of the New Testament, this first application of the phrase, in Jesus Christ: *Christ is the sphere of our justification,* with all that this involves: reconciliation, redemption, eternal life, safekeeping. In Him the sinner at once becomes, in God's sight, a saint, admitted to a new standing, not on the platform of law, but of grace. Outside of Christ, is alienation; inside this sphere, reconciliation; without, death; within, life; without, enmity; within, peace. By faith we are taken into Christ, made at once safe from holy wrath against sin, and kept safe from all perils and penalties. He, our divine Redeemer, becomes to us the new sphere of harmony and unity with God and His Law, with His life and His holiness.

As already intimated, each epistle has its own definite limits of application for the phrase, in Christ Jesus, and the divine truth which it conveys; and in each the range of thought is limited, in the main, by certain typical and representative events in the history and career of the God-man. In this epistle, it is to the *death, burial,* and *resurrection* of our Lord Jesus Christ, that the thoughts of the reader are preeminently directed, because these events belong together as forming the very foundation of

1 Dr. Handley C. G. Moule, of Cambridge, England, in his matchless commentary on Romans, thus translates verses 10 and 11: "Much more, being reconciled, we shall be kept safe in His life; and, not only so, but we shall be kept always rejoicing in God."

our justification. Compare chapter 4:25: "Who was delivered for our offenses and raised again for our justification." Here it is made unmistakably plain that the death and resurrection of Christ, together with the burial which lay between, accomplished the work of our justification. Death was the delivering over of our vicarious substitute and surety to the penalty of a broken law; burial was his committal to the grave, as dead; and resurrection was the deliverance from both death and Hades, as the divine sign and seal of His acceptance as our substitute and surety and of His vicarious atonement in our behalf.

We have heard of a Russian officer whose accounts could not be made to balance, and who feared that the merciless despotism of the empire would allow no room for leniency in dealing with him. While hopelessly poring over his "balance sheet" and in despair of ever making up his deficiency, it is said that he wrote, half inadvertently, on the paper before him: "Who can make good this deficit?" and fell asleep at his table. The czar passed, saw the sleeping officer, glanced curiously at the paper, and taking up the pen, wrote underneath: "I, even I, Alexander." The story may be a fiction, but it illustrates a far higher debt that is forever canceled. Does the hopeless sinner confront his awful bankruptcy and ask in despair, What can pay this my debt to a broken law? There is One who died and rose again, who from the cross of Calvary, the tomb in the garden, and the throne in heaven, answers, "I, even I, the Lord Jesus."

Let us then fix in our minds that the special horizon of this epistle is bounded by Christ's justifying work, and includes within its scope these three prominent facts: He died, He was buried, He rose again. All the great lessons here taught center about the cross and the sepulchre. Christ was the second and last Adam; the representative of the race; and so, judicially, he stands for the believer. In His death, the believing sinner is reckoned as having died for sin, and unto sin; in His burial, as having gone down into the grave, the place of death, decay, and corruption, there to leave as crucified, dead and buried, "the old man," the old nature, and the old life of sin, now forever "put off" in Christ, "the time past of our life sufficing to have wrought our own will;" and, in Christ's resurrection, the believer is counted by God as having come forth, "having put on the new man, which after God is created in righteousness and true holiness," endowed with a new Spirit of Life, henceforth to "walk in newness of life."

Hence it is that in chapter 5, Christ Jesus is set forth before us as the last Adam. The first Adam was the organic, ancestral, federal head of the race; his acts were representative acts, and, when he fell, the race which he represented fell in him—a truth which, when removed from the realm of mere polemic, controversial theology, is not difficult of apprehension; for it is plain that Adam could transmit to posterity no better nature or estate than he possessed. We, therefore, inherit his moral corruption and bankruptcy. In order to redeem the fallen race, God gave man a new Adam, another representative, the Lord Jesus Christ, all whose acts in behalf of man are, therefore, representative, not for Himself only, but for us for whom He stands in God's sight. Consequently, so far as we are, by faith in Him and by the new birth from above, identified with Him—as with Adam by sin and birth from beneath—*Christ's acts become our own.* This conception of representation threads the entire Bible, and is so important that it belongs among the fundamental truths of redemption. Only in the light of it can redemption be understood; but both condemnation and justification become divinely luminous in the light which it throws upon these two opposite positions of man before God.

We may take an illustration from a lower sphere. Here is a

man whose father's bankruptcy bankrupts the whole family, so that he with the others is overwhelmed in the general wreck of the family fortunes. There is, however, another party, it may be an uncle, or a grandparent, who, in this crisis, assumes all the liabilities, pays all debts, and thus redeems the family name and credit. Now, is it not plain, without argument, that, so far as this son is identified with his bankrupt father, he is himself financially ruined; but that, so far as he is identified with the party who pays the debts, he is, in the sight of the law, delivered from bankruptcy and financially justified?

This lesson finds typical illustration in the story of Ruth. So far as this Moabitish woman, as the widow of Mahlon, was identified with her first husband, she was involved in his losses and liabilities; but, when she became the wife of Boaz, the redeemer of her estate and the lord of the harvest, she and her inheritance were redeemed, and she became the sharer of his wealth and social standing. All illustrations fail in divine things; but we may get a glimpse, from some such point of view, of the philosophy of the plan of salvation. In Christ, we, who in Adam were condemned and alienated, are justified and reconciled.

The believer's vital union with Christ Jesus is set forth, with great clearness of statement, in chapter 6:4–11, where his identification with the Lord Jesus in His death, burial, and resurrection is so plainly declared, and its practical bearings are shown. Compare 2 Corinthians 13:4. "For though He was crucified through weakness, yet He liveth by the power of God. For we also are weak in Him, but we shall live with Him by the power of God toward you."

In this sixth chapter of Romans seven significant statements are noticeable, and upon them the whole argument hangs and turns:

1. Christ was raised from the dead by the glory of the Father.

that is, He was divinely quickened or made alive, so that His resurrection was a miracle.

2. We, as believers, are planted together with Him in the likeness of His resurrection; that is, we share in the very power of God which raised Him from the dead.

3. Our old man is crucified with Him; that is, the former sinful nature is judicially regarded as crucified, dead, buried, and left in the tomb of Christ.

4. That the body of sin might be destroyed, that henceforth we should not serve sin; that is, the power of sin as our master is practically broken, and we are released.

5. We believe that we shall also live with him. Surely, we are not to refer this only to our final resurrection; from *His* resurrection, onward, forevermore, our life is one with His.

6. Death hath no more dominion over Him, and so we in Him are delivered from all that dominion of sin which is implied in death as its judicial penalty. Compare verse 14.

7. In that He liveth, He liveth unto God; and to us also God is to be the source, channel, and goal of our new life, and so we are to manifest our unity with Him.

This teaching is so wonderful that it would be incredible were it not found in the inspired Scripture, and thus sealed with the authority of the Divine Teacher. It is manifestly a revelation from God, for it never would have entered into the heart of any mere man, untaught of God, to conceive it.

This reminds one of a most forcible utterance of Sir Monier Williams, Professor of Sanskrit in Oxford University, and, perhaps, the greatest living authority on all questions affecting the literature and faiths of the Orient. At an anniversary of the Church Missionary Society in London, some ten years ago, he delivered a most remarkable address, in which he said that, when he began investigating Hinduism and Buddhism, he began to believe in what is called the evolution and growth of religious thought. But he adds, and we give his own memorable words:

"I am glad of the opportunity of stating publicly, that I am persuaded I was misled by the attractiveness of such a theory, and that its main idea was erroneous. . . . And now I crave permission at least to give two good reasons for venturing to contravene the favorite philosophy of the day. Listen to me, ye youthful students of the so-called sacred books of the East: search them through and through, and tell me, do they affirm of Vyasa, of Zoroaster, of Confucius, of Buddha, of Mohammed, what our Bible affirms of the founder of Christianity,—that *He, a sinless man, was made sin?* Not merely that He is the eradication of sin, but that He, the sinless son of man, was himself made sin. Vyasa and the other founders of Hinduism, enjoined severe penances, endless lustral washings, incessant purifications, infinite repetitions of prayer, painful pilgrimages, arduous ritual, and sacrificial observances, all with the one idea of *getting rid of sin*. All their books say so. But do they say that the very men who exhausted every invention for the eradication of sin were themselves *sinless men made sin? . . .* This proposition put forth in our Bible stands alone; it is wholly unparalleled; it is not to be matched by the shade of a shadow of a similar declaration in any other book claiming to be the exponent of the doctrine of any other religion in the world.

"Once again, do these sacred books of the East affirm of Vyasa, of Zoroaster, of Confucius, of Buddha, of Mohammed, what our Bible affirms of the founder of Christianity, that He, a *dead and buried man, was made life?* Not merely that He is the giver of life, but that He, the dead and buried man, *is* life. . . . All I contend for is, that such a statement is absolutely unique; and I defy you to produce the shade of a shadow of a similar declaration in any other sacred book of the world. And bear in mind that these two matchless, unparalleled declarations are closely, intimately, indissolubly connected with the great central facts and doctrines of our religion: the incarnation, the crucifixion, the resurrection, the ascension of Christ.

"The two unparalleled declarations quoted by me from our Holy Bible make a gulf between it and the so-called sacred books of the East, which severs the one from the others utterly, hopelessly, and forever; not a mere rift which may be easily closed up, but a veritable gulf which can not be bridged over by any science of religious thought; yes, a bridgeless chasm which no theory of evolution can ever span."

Prof. Max Müller, in addressing the British and Foreign Bible Society, declared, in a similar strain, that "the one keynote of all these so-called sacred books is *Salvation by works.* Our own Holy Bible is from the beginning to the end a protest against this doctrine."

What Sir Monier Williams and Prof. Müller thus affirm of the Word of God, as to its unique and wholly unparalleled teaching, we may find illustrated especially in this epistle. Here, if anywhere, we have the Sinless One made sin for sinners, and the Dead One raised from the dead to become life to believers; and here, if anywhere, we have salvation by faith put in most vivid contrast with salvation by works.

We can not leave this thought without at least hinting at its apologetic and evidential value. The question can not but arise: Where did the writers of this Bible get conceptions so original and unique? The world of mankind was forty centuries old when the New Testament began to be constructed, when the earliest books first appeared in the primitive Church. At least five great world kingdoms had in their way carried civilization to remarkable heights of development: the Egyptian,

Assyrian-Babylonian, Persian, Greek, and Roman. Progress had not been along the lines of commerce, martial prowess, material grandeur, and imperial splendor, alone, but philosophy had won some of its proudest triumphs. The race had done much of its subtlest and most original thinking before the Nazarene began his career of teaching. Now, how can it be accounted for that a few humble fishermen of Judea, or even a trained Hebrew scholar who had the advantage of Roman citizenship and Greek culture, should have given to mankind *absolutely new ideas,* and those, too, on the most vital themes? How came it that such new and marvelous conceptions are found in the Word of God, and *nowhere else?*

There is but one explanation: The world was visited by the Son of God. He told of heavenly things. He revealed the mind of God on subjects hitherto unveiled. What He had heard in a celestial school—the University of God—what no scholar or philosopher of earth had even imagined—He testified, and some received His testimony and set to their seal, experimentally, that God is true. And so it comes to pass that the Bible—because it is what it claims to be, God's Word, conveying God's thought—gives us absolutely new ideas of the way of salvation, of the sinless sin bearer, of the Risen Lord of Life; and announces the simple terms whereby He becomes to the believer, the sphere of a new life—his Justifier, Reconciler, Savior.

Let us tarry at the threshold of our study of this theme, to praise Him who in the Gospel of Christ has brought to light, life, and immortality; who has made the cross of Calvary a tree of life, and the sepulchre in the garden a doorway of life, and the faith of a little child the condition of life, to every penitent and believing sinner. Toplady says:

"When Christ entered into Jerusalem the people spread garments in the way: when He enters into our hearts, we pull off our own righteousness, and not only lay it under Christ's feet but even trample upon it ourselves."

Let a quotation from another writer, referring to Isaiah 53:5, enforce this same lesson:

"Let every poor sinner, and let every preacher to sinners *put this great truth where God puts it*, in the very center and midst, as the most vital and important of all truths. How simple this verse which expresses it! It states FACTS, facts to which the prophet looked wonderingly forward, facts on which we look gratefully backward. HE, the mighty and the holy One, He was wounded, bruised, chastised! He was treated thus, not because *He deserved it,* but for *our sakes,* because *we* deserved it. His punishment is our peace. His stripes are our healing. His death our life. O greatest of all facts! well mayest Thou have the central place in prophecy, the central place in our hearts! This is the Gospel. To *believe* this is to be saved; He has borne the stripes and punishment due to each believer, who will, therefore, have *none* to bear. To believe this is to be happy, for it is to see a substitute in our place of doom and death, setting us free! To believe this is to be holy, for faith in such facts must make us *love* the One that suffered in our stead, and *hate* the sin that brought sore stripes on HIM. Brother, canst thou make it singular, and say, 'He was wounded for MY transgressions; He was bruised for MY iniquities; the chastisement of MY peace was upon Him, and with His stripes I am healed?'"

The 20th of January, 1896, marked the centenary of John Howard, the philanthropist, who went on his famous "circumnavigation of charity" to let light into the dungeons of the world's prisons. His was a life of singular self-sacrifice for others. Beginning amid the cottages of Cardington, and undertaking reforms among his own tenantry, his work grew wider until from the jails and prisons of Britain it embraced the cells of the imprisoned everywhere. In Bedford jail, where Bunyan had spent twelve years a century before, Howard found men and women, who were felons, living in a common day-room, their night-rooms being two dungeons "down steps." There was only a single courtyard for debtors and criminals, there was no apartment for the jailer, and the sanitary conditions bred fatal jail fever, which proved destructive also outside prison walls. Howard's whole soul was so moved that he "emptied himself" of all that mortals prize, to go on his wide mission of love, and become a servant of servants to the lowest and vilest classes.

The inscription on his monument is eloquently suggestive:

Vixit propter alios salvos fecit.

This was, indeed, the victory whereby he overcame. He lived for others, and he gave his life for their uplifting and salvation. He was so indifferent to fame that he forbade a project to build him a memorial. And, as Dean Milman says, "the first statue admitted to St. Paul's was not that of a statesman, warrior, or even of a sovereign; it was that of John Howard, the pilgrim, not to gorgeous shrines of saints and martyrs, not even to holy lands, but to the loathsome depths of darkness of the prisons of what called itself the civilized world."

Let us not forget where Howard learned his life lesson of philanthropy: it was from *One* of whom it was said, in taunt sublimely true:

"He saved others,
Himself He can not save."

The Son of God and Son of man gave Himself a ransom for many. It was by His death, burial, and resurrection that He made possible a *sphere of life* for you and me. Life for us was purchased by death for Him. And this first of New Testament epistles is the revelation of the first conditions of our salvation. His cross abolished our judgment; His burial abolished for us the fear of death and the grave; and his resurrection became to us alike the hope and the pledge of life, both for soul and body.

It is plain that to be in Christ Justified, is far more than Pardon or even Reconciliation; it includes being *counted as just, and put upon the same standing as Christ,* before God.

I

Summary of Teaching in Epistle to the Romans.

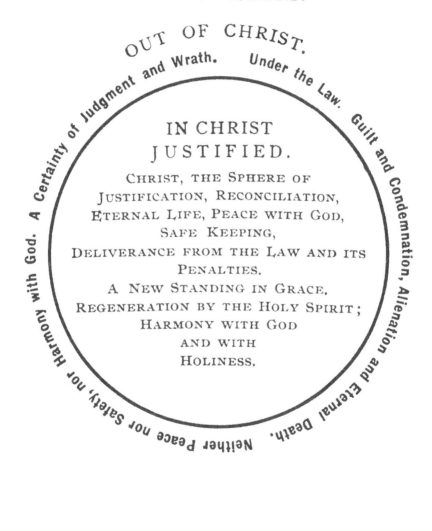

OUT OF CHRIST.

A Certainty of Judgment and Wrath. Under the Law. Guilt and Condemnation, Alienation and Eternal Death. Neither Peace nor Safety, nor Harmony with God.

IN CHRIST
JUSTIFIED.

Christ, the Sphere of
Justification, Reconciliation,
Eternal Life, Peace with God,
Safe Keeping,
Deliverance from the Law and its
Penalties.
A New Standing in Grace.
Regeneration by the Holy Spirit;
Harmony with God
and with
Holiness.

CHAPTER 2

THE EPISTLES TO THE CORINTHIANS

In the First Epistle, the first chapter and the second verse, we first meet the phrase which we seek: "SANCTIFIED IN CHRIST JESUS," and, according to the rule that has been found to be true, this proves upon examination to furnish us with the key-note of both of these epistles.

This thought is further amplified in the thirtieth verse of the same chapter, where, as from an exalted mountain peak, we seem to scan the whole horizon of our salvation and of the work of Christ. We are there taught that, being "in Christ Jesus," we find Him "made, of God, unto us wisdom, and righteousness, and sanctification, and redemption." But, in these epistles, sanctification in Christ Jesus is as prominent as justification in Christ Jesus has been found to be in the Epistle to the Romans. In the latter, the death of Christ was made most prominent; here, it is our life in Him and His life in us. There, our thoughts were directed mainly to His cross and passion; but here, it is to His Spirit, as bestowed upon the believer and dwelling in him. Or, to speak more accurately and carefully, the thought of the Apostle Paul begins, in the Epistles to the Corinthians, where, as we might say, it ends in the Epistle to the Romans. In the latter

epistle we follow Christ through His death and burial to His resurrection, when He comes forth from the grave endowed with
the Spirit of life. But the Epistles to the Corinthians start—may
we not say?—from His inbreathing of the Spirit into His disciples on the day of His resurrection and the subsequent indue-
ment of the disciples with the Spirit on the day of Pentecost.

We might compare the two epistles thus:

Romans: *Justified in Christ Jesus by His blood.*

Corinthians: *Sanctified in Christ Jesus by His Spirit.*

And, through both of the Epistles to the Corinthians, the
golden thread of connection is thus our union with Christ by
the indwelling and inworking of His Holy Spirit.

In First Corinthians (6:17) is the brief but grand statement
which illuminates and illustrates both of these letters:

"He that is joined to the Lord is one spirit."

In this language we have represented the highest conceivable
unity. The stones of the building may be removed; the branch
may be cut off from the vine, and the limb severed from the
body; the sheep may wander from the shepherd, the child from
the father; the bride may be divorced from the bridegroom; but
you can not divide spirit asunder. Therefore, when we are told
that "he that is *joined to the Lord is one Spirit,*" we have the
highest possible representation of unity—a unity which nothing
can dissolve.

In the First Epistle to the Corinthians this unity with the
Lord Jesus is exhibited as involving especially the following privileges and duties:

First. A new knowledge of God, or insight into Divine
things. (Chapter 2.)

Second. A new indwelling of God, we becoming His temple
(3:16), and hence a new possession of us by God.

Third. A new possession in God as our portion. (3:21–23.)

Fourth. A new stewardship in God, with corresponding obligation. (4:1–2.)

Fifth. A new separation unto God as His holy abode. (6:11–20.)

Sixth. A new sanctity even in secular toil, as a calling in which we abide with God. (7:20–24.)

Seventh. A new subjection, even of the body, to His glory. (9:27.)

Eighth. A new communion with God. (10:16–17.)

Ninth. A new service to God, made possible by communion with Him. (12.)

Tenth. A new dominion of love as the controlling power. (13.)

Eleventh. A new holiness and decorum in public assemblies. (14.)

Twelfth. A new victory over death and the grave. (15.)

This analysis is not, of course, exhaustive, but it serves, so far as we have carried it, to communicate to us how truly all the thoughts of these epistles revolve about the phrase we are considering, and the thought which it embodies.

To resume: Christ is here represented as the sphere of sanctification and personal holiness. Being in Him, we have in Him unity with God by the Holy Spirit, which Spirit becomes the new *element* or *atmosphere* of that life of which Christ is the *sphere*. We have thus a new knowledge of God and a new indwelling of God in us; we thus possess God and are possessed by Him, separate and subject unto Him, so that even our bodies partake of His life and immortality. As Romans deals largely with what we are by our entrance into God, in Corinthians we are confronted with what we are by God's entrance into us. There, it was the new sphere of life; here, it is the new atmosphere of life. There, we in Him; here, He in us.

In Second Corinthians, the same great thought is further expanded and enlarged. Take, for instance, the first chapter, from the twentieth to the twenty-second verses, where we are taught that in Him we are established, anointed, sealed, and have the earnest or foretaste of our future inheritance. The dominant thought here is the privilege we have in and through Christ. Paul makes very emphatic and prominent our transformation into His image (3:18); our new creation in Christ Jesus (5:17); our separation unto Him (6:14–7:1); our unselfish liberality as the fruit of our union with Him (chapters 8 and 9); our abundance of revelation in Him (chapter 12), etc.

Here, again, we have attempted no exhaustive analysis, but have only sought to hint at the contents of the epistle, or draw the outline of this wonderful range of thought.

In these two epistles, then, we have Christ as the sphere of our holiness, and privilege in Him; we have in Him everything else, and the very anticipation of heaven itself. We have conformity to His likeness, cleansing from sin, power over sin, fellowship with God, and revelations of the bliss of paradise, even while upon earth.

If, in these two epistles, any thought overtops the rest, it is that of the *new creation in Christ Jesus* (chapter 5:17), where the word "creature" should undoubtedly be rendered "creation." Compare Galatians 6:15. The parallel passage is in Revelation 21:5, where God says: "Behold, I make all things new." Here that is true of the *individual* which is there to be realized of the *whole creation*. We enter into Christ Jesus, and we have in Him the entrance into a new world, ourselves becoming a part of that new creation.

A careful comparison of Second Corinthians (6:17–7:1) with the twenty-first chapter of Revelation (3–5) will show how closely these two passages correspond.

Here, also, we see how and why Christ becomes to us the sphere of new *power* in becoming the sphere of new *life*. A sphere contains an atmosphere, and that atmosphere may be quite different from that which is outside; it may have different qualities, and be capable of supporting life in a far higher degree. So, what we could not do, outside of Christ, becomes both natural and possible in Him, because we have new appetites, desires, and affinities. The old passions, habits, bondage, are displaced by a new life, capacity, and freedom.

To clearly apprehend all this wonderful truth and freely enter into this privilege, is the ideal condition of a disciple. The idea of a new creation suggests to us also the kindred idea of a new *adaptation*, or *affinity for God*, on the part of the believer. Every form of animal existence, and even of vegetable existence, demands what we call its appropriate *element;* that is, a sphere of life with conditions which are necessary to its development, and even to its very subsistence and existence. We call the air the element of the bird, because the air and the bird are manifestly made for each other. We call the water the element of the fish for the same reason of mutual adaptation. The bird can not live in the water, and the fish can not live in the air. We observe that the bird has a breathing apparatus adapted to the atmosphere, and the fish has a breathing apparatus adapted to the water. If either were to exchange places with the other, there must be corresponding changes in its physical structure and adaptation; the bird, to live in the water, must have gills instead of lungs, and the fish to live in the air must have lungs instead of gills. So the bird's wings must change to fins and the fish's fins must change to wings. In fact, there would have to be changes in the whole structure, which it would be possible only for the Creator to effect. How wonderfully analogous to the case of the disciple! In order to enter into Christ Jesus and to exist in the new atmosphere which we find in this new sphere of life, that atmosphere must become our element; and there must be changes, which correspond to structural changes, which must take place in our very mental and moral constitution. As it were, the lungs must change to gills, or the gills to lungs. This is what we call "the new birth, or regeneration." So far as we are concerned, the act by which we enter into Christ is the act of repentance and faith, repentance being the leaving of the old sphere of life behind us, and faith being the entrance into the new sphere. But there must be a divine act, corresponding to our human act—an act of regeneration on God's part, corresponding to the act of appropriation on our part; otherwise, even if it were possible for us to enter into the new sphere, we should find ourselves unable to live or abide in it. *This is the mystery of the new birth.*

If any man be in Christ, he is by necessity a new creation. He must be born from above, born again, born of the Spirit, enabled to breathe the new atmosphere and live in the new element. Whether the human act or the divine act has the precedence, we are neither concerned to inquire, nor are we capable to determine. There is a profound mystery about the whole subject upon which the Word of God sheds no decisive light; but the paradox is not a contradiction, nor does the mystery involve an absurdity. It is sufficient for us to know that we shall never enter into Christ save by our own consent, and to know with equal certainty that we shall never enter into Christ without God's new creative act.

Here we must leave the mystery, while we bless God for the privilege.

It will be seen by any thoughtful student of the Holy Scriptures how grand and important is the truth which thus meets us in these two Epistles to the Corinthians. The indwelling of God in Christ is the full, final, and most complete argument for, and exhibition of, that doctrine of separation, which runs from Genesis to Revelation, throughout the entire Scripture. We may say that there are at least seven stages in the development of this doctrine:

First. Separation by covenant, as when Abraham was called out from his country and his kindred. (See Genesis 12:1–7.)

Second. Separation by divine fellowship, so exquisitely presented in Exodus (33:14–16). Moses represents the fact that God's presence goes with His people as the one fact that separates himself and the people from all the others that are upon the face of the earth.

Third. Separation by ordinances. See Leviticus 20:24–26 where three times God addresses His people as a separated people, and makes the ceremonial distinction and difference between clean and unclean beasts, fowls and reptiles, to be the outward sign of this separation.

Fourth. Separation by vow, as in the case of the Nazarite, in the sixth chapter of Numbers, where four conditions are made prominent:

(1) The suppression of appetite.

(2) Indifference to public custom.

(3) Absolute withdrawal from death or corruption.

(4) Supreme loyalty to God over all human kindred.

Fifth. Separation by obedience as presented in the entire book of Deuteronomy. (Compare Chapter 7.)

Sixth. Separation by wedlock or espousal. See Jeremiah 3:14: "I am married unto you." Compare Ezekiel 16. Compare also Ephesians 5:25–33, where this doctrine of the divine espousal of His people in Christ is expanded and applied.

Seventh. But, when we come to the Epistles of the Corinthians, we have the last and greatest of all the modes of separation:

The indwelling of God in the believer by the Holy Ghost, which makes man God's habitation, temple, holy of holies! There are two ways in which a man shows himself to be the owner of a house: First, by purchase; second, by occupation. He buys the dwelling, and then he enters into it and lives in it. And these are the two ways in which God is represented as making the believer His special dwelling-place: First, ye are bought with a price; second, the Spirit of God dwelleth in you. There can be no separation more unmistakable than this. *We have been purchased by redeeming blood for the habitation of God through the Spirit, and through the Spirit God actually does indwell in every true believer.*

Such indwelling of God should insure the holiness of the believer. Walter Scott wrote of a certain acquaintance: "I can not tolerate that man; and it seems to me as if I hated him for things not only past and present, but for some future offense which is as yet in the womb of fate." The Holy Ghost's inhabitation should leave no possibility of actual sinning nor room even for the thought of sin. And where is such cleanness of soul to come from, apart from Christ? "By no political alchemy," Herbert Spencer tells us, "can you get golden conduct out of leaden instincts." The power to set the heart right, to renew the springs of action, comes from Christ through the Holy Spirit.

We thus reach the second stage of our journey through these paths of God's truth. And we here find Jesus Christ our Lord presented as the sphere of the believer's holy living—his sanctification as well as justification, his higher salvation from *sin* as well as from sin's penalty. Salvation is not by character, but it is not independent of character. Heaven is not and can not be the home of saved souls, if it be not also the abode of sanctified souls. God could have nothing less than a *clean* house where He lives. Nothing defiled or defiling can enter there; and He, whom the Epistle to the Romans shows as the secret of our entrance into a justified state, is here revealed to us as inbreathing the very Spirit and Life of God, whereby we are made partakers of the Divine nature, and thereby possible partakers of the Divine bliss.

II

SUMMARY OF TEACHING IN EPISTLE TO THE CORINTHIANS.

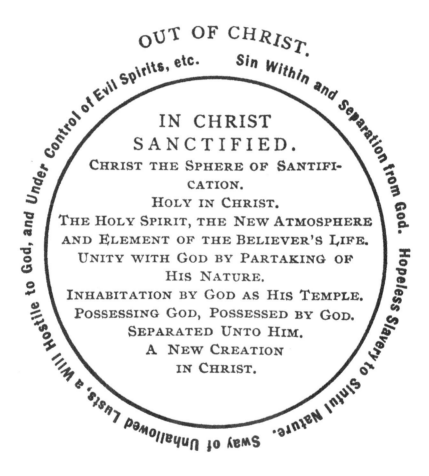

OUT OF CHRIST.

Sin Within and Separation from God. Hopeless Slavery to Sinful Nature. Sway of Unhallowed Lusts, a Will Hostile to God, and Under Control of Evil Spirits, etc.

IN CHRIST SANCTIFIED.

CHRIST THE SPHERE OF SANTIFI-
CATION.
HOLY IN CHRIST.
THE HOLY SPIRIT, THE NEW ATMOSPHERE
AND ELEMENT OF THE BELIEVER'S LIFE.
UNITY WITH GOD BY PARTAKING OF
HIS NATURE.
INHABITATION BY GOD AS HIS TEMPLE.
POSSESSING GOD, POSSESSED BY GOD.
SEPARATED UNTO HIM.
A NEW CREATION
IN CHRIST.

Chapter 3

THE EPISTLE TO THE GALATIANS

Of this epistle, chapter first, and chapter second, as far as verse 14, are historical and introductory, and the proper argument of the epistle is not fully entered upon until this preliminary or prefatory portion is passed. But, so soon as we touch the body of the epistle proper, we find the phrase *in Christ* or its equivalent, *with Christ*, abounding. See 2:15–20.

Not only does the relation of the believer to Christ, as the sphere of his being, again appear here, as the controlling thought of this epistle, but in no equal number of words found anywhere else is the subject presented with such completeness and comprehensiveness. Every variety of expression is here found, such as "by the faith of Christ," "crucified with Christ," etc.; but the most striking words which arrest the eye are these: *"I live, yet not I, but Christ liveth in me."*

Here is the key to the Epistle to the Galatians: "IN CHRIST CRUCIFIED, YET LIVING UNTO GOD." As a believer I am in Christ, and therefore I am dead to the *law* and to its penalty; I am in Christ, and therefore alive unto God, and dead to the *world* (6:14) and to the old *self-life,* and to the power of the *flesh.* (5:24.)

There are thus four aspects of the crucifixion—in a sense a four-fold crucifixion of the believer: he dies to the *law* both as a justifier and an accuser; he dies to the *world* with its fascination and domination; he dies to the *flesh* with its affections and lusts; and he dies to *himself* that Christ may live in him.

The full significance of this teaching will be seen only when the exact language is carefully noted, even to the changes of voice, mood, and tense in the verb, and of prepositions which here are to be found in great variety. To begin with the prepositions: in verses 19–20 of chapter two, we have in the English version seven prepositions: through, to, unto, with, in, by, for; and in the Greek three, δια, εν, υπερ; others being suggested by the case of nouns and by the construction of the sentence, and which the English translation admirably renders by the seven prepositions there found. But let us notice also the changes of verbs: "I am dead," or, "I died" (R. V.); "I am crucified," or, "I have been crucified" (R. V.); "the world is crucified," or "hath been crucified unto me" (R. V.); and, "have crucified the flesh." One can not but observe the marked change in the last case, where we have not the *passive* but *active* voice; and not without reason. For in part our crucifixion with Christ is *judicial, constructive, passive,* belonging wholly to the past and completed work of the cross; but in part it is practical, actual, destructive of a present power and enemy; and active, as something in which we take active part. So far as the law is concerned, I have nothing to do as a believer but to accept Christ's satisfaction of its claims by His death, and His purchase of my justification by His obedience. The whole transaction is as much a past one as a canceled debt or a ransom paid. I, through the law, which brought Him to the cross as the sinner's satisfaction and surety, died, in Him, to the law, both as my vindicator and accuser. And so, in His death, with which by faith I am identified, the world is for evermore made my enemy because it was His, and I am in Him exposed to its derision as was He. To be in Christ implies that I am no more in the world as the sphere of my true life, love, and satisfaction. This again is a past transaction, tho it may become more and more a practical reality as I come more under the power of that transaction. But, as to the flesh with its affections and lusts, is not that a daily dying to which I consent as a *present fact*, and which implies *present pain?* The faith whereby I am made one with Christ as the sinbearer implies no participation in His vicarious agony. He suffered for me, the just for the unjust, that He might bring me unto God. But I did not suffer with Him on the cross, nor in any sense share that vicarious death, save as He was my substitute that I might not come into judgment. He bore my sins that I might not bear them; and from the moment of my full acceptance of Him as my Savior and Substitute and Surety, my penalty is borne and my judgment is past.

Not so of this *flesh* crucifixion. It is something to which I consent as a present experience. It has to do, not with a justification which He bought for me and which I afterward accepted, without participation in the process; but with a sanctification that is wrought in me by the indwelling Spirit and which I am now to participate in, working out my own salvation with fear and trembling, knowing that it is God that worketh in me both to will and to do. This is the mortifying of our members which are upon the earth, referred to in Romans 8:13 and in Colossians 3:5: "Mortify therefore your members." Mortify does not mean to *reckon* dead but to *make* dead. Here is a daily, practical, painful death which by the Spirit we in a sense *inflict* on ourselves, not in any meritorious sort, but as a matter of choice, that we may be actually identified with Christ in holy living and serving, as we are judicially one with Him in the justifying efficacy and effect of His crucifixion.

Thus the Epistle to the Galatians meets the believer where the Epistles to the Romans and to the Corinthians leave him, and urges him forward. It is the epistle of "newness of life," corresponding to His *forty days' walk* after His resurrection. How beautiful, and how significant! In Romans, we saw the believer in Christ expiating the law's penalty and satisfying its claims, dying, buried, and then rising by the power of the Spirit, prepared to live unto God. In Corinthians, we saw him inbreathed and indwelt of the Spirit and finding in the Spirit his divine element, the source and secret of continuous life and permanent and indissoluble union with Christ. And now the Epistle to the Galatians opens up before the believer a *complete life walk*, corresponding to the path which the risen Christ pursued between the sepulchre and the ascension. That walk of His in newness of life covered *forty days*, the period of completeness, and it stands for the rounded-out life of the believer, after he is risen with Christ and has received the Holy Spirit, whose indwelling makes such a "walk" with God, in the Spirit, possible.

For this reason it is that *nowhere else* but in this epistle do we find the *four foes of the holy life, all put before us in their relations to Christ's cross.*

First of all the *law,* which is our foe, because its voice is always and justly condemnatory. Turn which way we will for legal justification, it meets us only as an accuser. If we attempt to atone for our past disobedience, it reminds us that there can no possible amends be made by us, because disobedience is death, and we are *dead* to God and to all hope—we have not even *life* in us to become the basis of fellowship with God. Or, if we attempt to start anew, henceforth to obey, the law reminds us that the sin of the past would make our acceptance impossible, even if we could henceforth perfectly keep the commandments of God; and, moreover, that such obedience is impossible because of the *sin* which is the very root not only of all our sins, but of our depraved *being* or nature itself. But the law is slain as our enemy, for when Christ died for us, He put the law power out of court, so far as our judgment is concerned, so that even the law can no longer lay anything to the charge of God's elect.

But there is a second foe: the *world;* and what shall I do to meet that and overcome it? This is the victory that overcometh the world, even our faith. He has overcome the world, and He bids us be of good cheer. John 16:33. We have only to accept our justified standing in Him and reckon on His death for us and His life in us, and the power of the world is broken. Because it was and is His enemy, it is also *ours;* but because it was and is His *vanquished* foe, it is also our subdued, defeated, overcome foe. The powers of the age to come we have tasted, and the powers of the present evil age are driven back, and so a second foe is defeated. We look at the unseen and eternal, rather than the seen and temporal, and walk by faith, not by sight.

But there is a third foe of our spiritual life and holy walk, and how shall we meet it? It is the *flesh,* with its affections and lusts warring against the Spirit with the aspirations and affinities for God which the Spirit makes possible. Here again we are crucified with Christ. We take our stand at the cross and consent to be nailed to it, voluntarily, actually; to submit to the pain whereby the flesh dies; the hands are pierced that carnal work may no longer be done in the energy of the flesh; the feet are pierced that no longer we may walk according to the flesh; the brow is pierced with the thorn-crown that our head may not any longer be held up for human diadems and fading laurel wreaths; the side is pierced that the heart may relinquish its fleshly energy and preference, and be occupied with God. This is, let us not deny it! a painful process—it is the voluntary and daily crucifixion of the fleshly affections and lusts. And so, but only so, is a third foe defeated by the cross, which *we take up daily*, that we may follow Him.

Another foe remains, subtlest of all—the *self-life*. What a host of foes in one! The self-trust that prevents trust only in Him,—the self-help that turns us from our only true Help,—the self-love that makes our own advantage an idolatrous object,—the self-pride that absorbs us in our own supposed excellence,—the self-defense that makes us our own champions and promotes endless strife,—the self-glory that puts even the glory of God in the background.

What shall be done with the self-life? Let us learn here that the only hope again is in being crucified with Christ. On the cross His self-life, though never corrupted by sin, was given up for others. He gave *Himself* for us. And He says to us, if any man will come after me, let him *deny himself*—not his self-indulgences, which may only change their form—but him*self*. Much that we call self-denial is not *self*-denial at all. We cut off some branch of our selfish enjoyments, but the only effect is to throw back the sap into the other branches to make them more vigorous and fruitful. The ax must be laid at the root of the tree; that is denial of *self*. And then, as Dr. Moule beautifully says, the great gigantic, arrogant, nominative *"I"* is "inflected into the prostrate, humble, objective *me"*—"I am crucified with Christ. Nevertheless *I live, yet not I*, but *Christ liveth in me."*

There remains but one more *foe*—the devil—and we shall see that his defeat is presented to us, not in this epistle, but in the Epistle to the Ephesians; and for the obvious reason that *that* victory is connected not so much with the *death* of Christ as with His *ascension* to the heavenlies. Here we have to do with those foes of holy living whose defeat is particularly associated with His *cross*. I am *crucified* with Christ, and hence I am dead to the law, I am crucified to the world, I have crucified the flesh, and the self-life is nailed to the cross that the *I* might no longer be active but passive—the *me* in whom He dwells and works. I can not be crucified to the devil, nor can I crucify him; even to the crucified disciple he appears as a wily foe, constantly on the alert, and we need to mount with Christ to the heavenlies before Satan is beneath our feet.

What wonder, then, that in Galatians 6:15, as in 2 Corinthians 5:17, we have Christ presented as the sphere of the *new creation*. In Christ Jesus neither circumcision nor uncircumcision availeth anything, but a *new creation;* no forms, ceremonies, rites, regulations of the outer life can effect or affect the new position in Christ. We enter into Him by faith, and find that we are in a sphere where *all things are new.*

No law thunders its alarms there: we are on Zion, not underneath Sinai. The world makes no appeal there, for its gold would be trodden under feet as refuse, and its crowns are all seen to be withered and worthless. The flesh has no control there, for the law of the Spirit of life controls the whole being. The old self sways us no longer, for what used to exalt itself against God and usurp authority, is content to be servant of servants to Him. We are in Christ, in a new world of privilege and possession. Like Him in His forty days' walk we are living a *supernatural* life, a life more in heaven than on earth, a life in the power of the Spirit, a life which defies all the old forces that swayed us, as He was no longer under the limitations of the human and the natural. The new walk with God in Christ is a walk in an essentially new world of dependence on God and of power in God. Of course, no rites will avail to introduce us into such a new world—renewal alone would suffice.

Here, then, we have found Christ the sphere of a new life which comes to us by the surrender of the old. We cease from all dependence on the law that we may know the power of grace.

We cease from all dependence on the flesh that we may walk in the Spirit, and no longer fulfil its lusts. We cease from walking with the world that we may walk with God, and we resign the self-life that the Christ-life may be fully regnant in us.

This epistle suggests a possible and practical walk with God. But its secret is a new *atmosphere of life*. There is a displacement of a hostile element, that once made holy living impossible, by another element which, so far as it prevails, renders deliberate sinning quite as impossible.

"Walk by the Spirit, and ye shall not fulfil the lust of the flesh. For the flesh lusteth against the Spirit, and the Spirit against the flesh; for these are contrary the one to the other; that ye may not do the things that ye would." Galatians 5:16–17. R. V.

Rev. F. B. Meyer says:

"In the best of men there is a tendency to do certain things they ought not, but the more they are filled with the Spirit, the more it is true of them that they are kept from doing what otherwise they would. When I was a boy I used to go to the Polytechnic in London, where my favorite diversion was a div-ing-bell, which had seats around the rim, and which at a given time was filled with people and lowered into a tank. We used to go down deeper, deeper into the water, but not a drop came into that diving-bell, tho it had no bottom, and the water was quite within reach, because the bell was so full of air that, tho the water lusted against the air, the air lusted against the water, because air was being pumped in all the time from the top, and the water could not do what it otherwise would do. If you are full of the Holy Ghost, the flesh-life is underneath you, and tho it would surge up, it is kept out."

To one who walks in the Spirit, the lusts of the flesh become impotent to control, until the spiritual man comes at last to marvel that he ever felt certain inclinations and passions swaying him. Let us once more hear the old eastern story:

"The haughty favorite of an Oriental monarch threw a stone at a poor priest. The dervish did not dare to throw it back, for the favorite was very powerful. So he picked up the stone and put it carefully in his pocket, saying to himself: 'The time for revenge will come by and by, and then I will repay him.' Not long afterward, walking in one of the streets, he saw a great crowd, and found to his astonishment, that his enemy, the favorite, who had fallen into disgrace with the king, was being paraded through the principal streets on a camel, exposed to the jests and insults of the populace. The dervish seeing all this, hastily grasped at the stone which he carried in his pocket, saying to himself: 'The time for my revenge has come, and I will repay him for his insulting conduct.' But after considering a moment, he threw the stone away, saying: *The time for revenge never comes;* for if our enemy is powerful, revenge is dangerous as well as foolish, and if he is weak and wretched, then revenge is worse than foolish, it is mean and cruel. And in all cases it is forbidden and wicked.'"

Not only for revenge, but for all voluntary sin, the time should never come to a regenerated child of God. The believer, having received the Spirit of God as the *indwelling* Spirit, must accept Him practically as the *inworking* Spirit, and follow His gentlest and faintest motions and leadings. There is something higher than even to be *taught* by the Spirit, namely, to be *led* of the Spirit. We fear many have been taught who have not been led; and failure to be led makes us more and more incapable of being taught, for the disobedient soul becomes callous to divine impression. He who is risen with Christ, and has the Breath of God in him, should live as a risen, quickened, breathing son of God, and *walk in* the Spirit in newness of life.

This expression, first found in Romans 6:4, is one of singular meaning, and the whole Epistle to the Galatians is a commentary upon it. Let us, therefore, tarry to examine it more carefully. "That, *like as Christ was raised from the dead by the glory of the Father, even so we also should walk in newness of life.*"

Two things here are very noticeable. First, there is to be a walk in newness of life, and, second, it is to find its type and likeness in the resurrection life of the Lord Himself.

This phrase, "newness of life," occurs only here, and itself opens up an immense territory of thought. Even in the life of the God-man there was, after His rising from the dead, a *newness of life manifested*, which is the type and pattern of what our life may be and ought to be in Him.

We observe apparently *new conditions* in our Lord's post-resurrection life on earth. Up to this time Christ had a mortal body, born of a woman, made under the law, and subject to human limitations, identified with the condition of humanity. Death was possible to that body, and actually endured by Him as part of His humiliation. But, after the resurrection, when He rose to die no more, and death had no more dominion over Him, He was, indeed, the "Prince of Life."

His life was now and henceforth a resurrection life. He was "declared to be the Son of God with power, according to the Spirit of Holiness, by the resurrection from the dead."

It was a supernatural life. His rising was a miracle. If the Scriptures are very minutely examined, it will be found that He appears to have come forth without human or even angelic aid. Tho the angel rolled back the stone from the door of the sepulchre, it is never once intimated that Christ waited for that before He left the sealed tomb; it would rather appear that He emerged from that closed tomb as one who could not be thus holden. And so there is more than an intimation that He sloughed off those grave wrappings, and left them in their original convolutions, undisturbed, as they were wrapped or rolled about Him. This was what convinced John that the resurrection was miraculous. He saw the long linen cloths—which, with a hundred pounds of spices, had been tightly wrapped about His body and His head—lying on the floor of the rock tomb, exactly as He had been enveloped in them—His body, endowed with resurrection power, slipping out from these tight and heavy cerements of the grave, because they could not hold Him fast. See John 20:7–8. Observe the word, ɛντɛτυλιγμɛνον. And all through those forty days Christ seems to have been independent of former conditions and limitations. He entered within closed doors, He assumed different forms, He appeared instantly and as instantly vanished; and finally ascended as one whom even gravitation no more controlled.

All this suggests what is meant by our walking in newness of life, and why such a simile is connected with it, "that, like as Christ was raised from the dead," etc. Our life in Him should be a life subject to entirely new conditions—essentially a resurrection life, a life supernatural in power, possible only by the Spirit of Holiness, a life no longer under the dominion of former lusts, fleshly bondage; essentially a divine life, in which celestial forces prevail; a life of heavenly knowledge, and strength, and peace, and patience, and power; a life of heavenly frames, having the lamb-like, dove-like quality. Our resurrection life may be and should be like His, more of heaven than of earth, a mysterious life that no worldly man or worldly-minded disciple can understand or explain.

This epistle contains an instructive allegory or parable, that of Hagar and Ishmael, the pertinency of which is not seen by every reader. Let us close this chapter by a reference to it.

In chapter 4:22–31, this history is presented as having a deeper allegorical meaning than the mere surface reveals. This

Hagar is Mount Sinai, which gendereth to bondage. Sarah represents grace, and Isaac, her son, the liberty of faith. Hagar represents law, and Ishmael, who is her son, represents the bondage which unbelief engenders. The territory in which both for a time sought to live is the believer's own experience. But the two are incompatible and irreconcilable. Faith and unbelief, liberty and slavery, love and fear, hope and despair, can not abide together. And God says to every child of His, "cast out the bondwoman and her son, for there can be no common inheritance for the son of the bondwoman and the son of the freewoman. Give your heart wholly to the dominion of grace and faith."

The same lesson is taught in Hebrews 12:18–29, in that other parable of Sinai and Sion. Leave the mount that quakes and burns, with its blackness and darkness and tempest and trumpet and awful voice of law; and live on Mount Sion, the place of the king's palace, with its holy memories, experiences, and prospects. There you look back to Calvary's cross, up to heaven's daily blessing, and forward to the far but near horizon of the blessed hope. Faith reconciles; faith saves, not only from hell, but from the inward slough of despond and the torments of fear. Faith makes real the encampment of God's holy angels about the believer and the fellowship of all redeemed souls in heaven and earth. Faith makes you conscious and confident of your heavenly citizenship, and your interest in atoning blood, which calls not for vengeance but for mercy.

All these lessons are summed up in that one verse: "That, like as Christ was raised from the dead by the glory of the Father, even so we also should walk in newness of life."

III

Summary of Teaching in Epistle to the Galatians.

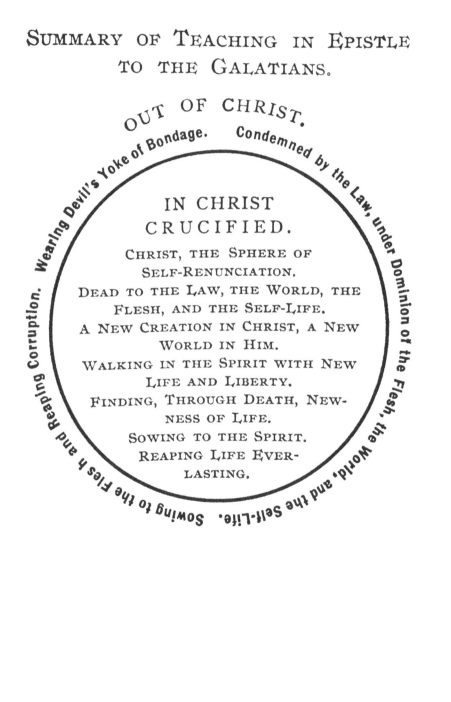

OUT OF CHRIST.

Wearing Devil's Yoke of Bondage. Condemned by the Law, under Dominion of the Flesh, the World, and the Self-Life. Sowing to the Flesh and Reaping Corruption.

IN CHRIST CRUCIFIED.

Christ, the Sphere of Self-Renunciation.
Dead to the Law, the World, the Flesh, and the Self-Life.
A New Creation in Christ, a New World in Him.
Walking in the Spirit with New Life and Liberty.
Finding, Through Death, Newness of Life.
Sowing to the Spirit.
Reaping Life Everlasting.

CHAPTER 4

THE EPISTLE TO THE EPHESIANS

The very first verse contains the expression, *"faithful in Christ Jesus,"* and the third verse furnishes the key to this epistle in one short sentence, comprising the sum of all its exalted teaching: *"Who hath blessed us with all spiritual blessings* IN THE HEAVENLIES IN CHRIST."

This letter to the Ephesians lifts us to the very summit, the third heaven of privilege, and is especially rich in that phrase which we are now devoutly tracing throughout the New Testament. We find here at least *ten* separate uses or combinations of the words *in Christ* or *in Him*, as applied to the present estate of the believer, and as exhibiting His possible heavenly life even while on earth; and there is *one* besides which refers to *coming* blessing. These features of this Epistle we shall find singularly true also of the companion Epistle to the Colossians.

In this epistle we are declared to be, IN CHRIST, chosen, predestinated to the adoption of children, accepted; to have redemption and forgiveness, to be quickened or made alive, raised, seated in the heavenlies; to have been sealed and to have obtained an inheritance: these are the ten present blessings, and the one, yet future, is that in Him we are to be gathered together in one, with all saints, at His coming.

The peculiar truth thus introduced to our view in this epistle is, therefore, the *heavenly nature and divine fullness* of this sphere of the new life. When by faith we enter into Christ, the life we are introduced into, is not earthly, but essentially heavenly. It is not to be confounded with joys and privileges which are of this world, however pure and lawful. In Christ we are lifted above the level even of saintly communion as such. Our human ties and relations with God's own people are very precious, but that of which the Spirit here treats is something higher than the human relation which disciples sustain here to each other. We ascend in thought above the Church on earth, with its assemblies of saints, its sacraments, ordinances, and fellowship; here we are viewed as *one with Christ and one in Christ*. He, indeed, in heaven, and we on earth; yet our life in Him a heavenly life because it is in Him who is in heaven. Hence the word *"places"* supplied by the translators, may mislead, for we are not as yet in heavenly places, but in earthly places, though we may and ought to be in heavenly *states* of mind, heart, and experience.

The difference is not a mere verbal distinction. A devout woman whom I once visited, to condole with her on the recent departure of an aged and most saintly mother, said to me with a smile: "For forty years, my dear mother's *mind* has been in Heaven." And I could not but recall those exquisite lines of Goldsmith:

> Like some tall cliff that lifts its awful form,
> Swells from the vale but midway leaves the storm,
> Though round its breast the rolling clouds are spread,
> Eternal sunshine settles on its head.

While yet in the body and on earth, the mind and heart

may be in Heaven; we ought to be essentially living on a higher, celestial level. This is the grand possibility and privilege to which the Holy Spirit turns our eyes. And, as all saints are, alike, in Christ Jesus, they are all in Him *one*. This thought of *our unity* in Christ runs side by side with the other, of our high privilege in Him, throughout these chapters: in fact, this unity is itself one of the most exalted forms of this heavenly life, and is more emphasized here than perhaps anywhere else, more figures being here employed to give it expression than in the whole New Testament besides.

Let us first of all glance at the teachings here contained as to this *unity of saints in Christ Jesus*.

To begin with, the conception of Christ, as the sphere of all holy living, implies this unity. This sphere is invisible, however real, and our entrance into it and our abiding in it are not therefore matters of sense. Our place in it has to be obtained or received through the Spirit's working, and recognized or perceived through the Spirit's teaching. We must also recognize the place of other saints in the same sphere, by the same spiritual discernment. As we come into contact with true fellow-believers and perceive in them the Christ image—as we see that they breathe the same air and live the same life, that they also belong to Christ and partake also of His Spirit, our conception of the unity of all believers in Him grows continually in vividness of impression. We can not help our love going out to them; to whatever different sphere they may belong, in family, social, or national life, they belong with us to that supreme sphere which is celestial and eternal. And here is the only real hope of unity in the Church: it is found in the recognition of our mutual relation to Christ, and in Him to each other—as our Lord prayed, "that they also may be *one in Us.*"

The spheres of family life, social life, church life, and national life are all *visible*, and they impress us with a vivid sense of our unity, as brothers, neighbors, fellow church members, fellow citizens: but, to a true child of God, the *invisible* bond that unites all believers to Christ is far more tender, and lasting, and precious; and, as we come to recognize and realize that we are all dwelling in one sphere of life in Him, we learn to look on every believer as our brother, in a sense that is infinitely higher than all human relationships. This is the one and only way to bring disciples permanently together. All other plans for promoting the unity of the Church have failed. Let us live more and more in Christ, and then we shall and must live more and more in the bonds of a holy love and peace. It must be first of all the unity of the Spirit.

This *unity in Christ* is so prominent in this epistle that we must not lightly pass it by. Besides the general conception of Christ as the sphere of holy life, common to all these epistles, we shall find the following other figures used here to express the same thought:

1. The *body* of which He is the head and we the members. 1:22, 23; 2:16; 4:12–16.

2. God's *workmanship*—ποιημα—same word as in Romans 1:20, a *creation* with a definite purpose, or object, and we, all, parts of that sphere of creation—"God's poem," 2:10.

3. A *commonwealth*, 2:12—πολιτεια—a community in which we are citizens, introduced into it by the blood. 2:19.

4. A *temple*, with the middle wall of partition broken down. 2:14. "He is our peace." Two *courts*—one.

5. *One new man*, 2:15, a very remarkable expression, ενα καινον ανθρωπον, nowhere else used.

6. One *household* of God, 2:19, οικειοι, members of one household.

7. One *building* or temple, in this case with reference to the

one foundation, etc., and one habitation of God through the Spirit. 2:20, 22.

8. *Fellow-heirs*. 3:6. Three words: συνκληρονομα—συσσωμα—συμμετοχα, participators of one inheritance.

9. *Family*, πατρια. 3:15. Tribe or race from one father—an amplification and expansion of the idea of one household.

10. One *body* and one *Spirit*, 4:4. The septiform of unity is contained in chapter 4, one body, one Spirit, one hope, one Lord, one faith, one baptism, one God and Father.

11. The *bride* or wife. 5:22–32.

12. The *panoply*. 6:10 and the following verses. All true believers are wearing the same armor, and panoplied in the same Divine power.

This unity with Christ and in Him is in this epistle made to depend on our partaking of His Spirit, and hence the prominence of the Holy Spirit, to whom the references are very frequent and varied:

1:13. That Holy Spirit of promise whereby we are sealed.

1:17. The Spirit of wisdom and revelation in the knowledge of Him.

1:19, 20. The Spirit of power who wrought in Christ and raised Him from the dead.

2:18. The Spirit of access, by whom we have access to the Father.

2:22. The Spirit of inhabitation whereby God dwells in us.

3:5. The Spirit of revelation of the mystery of Christ.

3:16. The Spirit of strength and might in the inner man.

4:4. The Spirit of unity in the body.

5:9. The Spirit of fruitfulness in all goodness, etc.

5:18. The Spirit of fullness, making all our life spiritual.

6:17. The Spirit of truth whose sword is the Word.

6:18. The Spirit of supplication and intercession.

Thus there are at least twelve or thirteen references to the Spirit of God.

Here, then, is the added teaching of the Epistle to the Ephesians, as compared with the preceding:

Christ is the sphere of all heavenly *privilege and blessing*. We have first of all *fellowship with Him*, so that, as He is so are we in this world. We are so in Him that God looks on us only as in Him, as having been and done and borne and achieved all that He has, Himself. In Him we are God's elect, accepted, forgiven, redeemed, raised from the dead, sealed as His own, and seated with Him, in the heavenlies.

Our fellowship is thus with the Father, in Him, as close as His own fellowship.

And our fellowship is also with all saints in heaven and on earth, of time, past, present, and future. We all belong, in Him, to Him and to one another, and the more we know Him, the more we shall know and love all who are His and who are in Him.

If there be anything higher than this, it is the *heavenly life* involved in all this teaching. We are *already* in heaven, so far as this becomes *real* to us, and have the earnest or foretaste of the one final inheritance of all saints.

For example, take chapter 6:10 and following. In our wrestling against the powers of darkness that encompass us round in the sphere of the *earthly*, what a refuge to be consciously environed by the *heavenly!* to feel Christ as *between* us and all hostile principalities and powers. Observe, however close our foes may be, the *panoply is between us and them*. And so it is of the believer. Christ is the panoply of our warfare. He is next us and between us and all our foes. How elaborately this thought is wrought out in this chapter. The powers of darkness are here represented in a *sixfold* aspect, as assailing the head, the heart, the vital parts, and the feet, and as needing to be met by an all-encompassing coat of mail.

How are they to be confronted? Only in Christ. He is to be the hope of salvation, and so a helmet for the head; He is to be our righteousness, and so a breastplate; He is to be our truth, and so a girdle that holds us and embraces us; He is to be our sandals, and so alacrity for our feet; He is to be the sword of our defense and offense, and the shield that quenches all the fiery darts of Satan.

We have, therefore, Christ here presented, not only as the heavenly sphere of fellowship with God and with saints, but as the sphere of absolute security from all foes.

There is added one word of warning. It is amazing that the epistle which thus reveals our highest privilege should close with the most terrible caution against Satanic wiles. Here where the *Spirit of God* is most conspicuous as the indwelling power of the believer, the *spirit of evil* is the most conspicuous as the spirit that worketh in the children of disobedience.

Why is this warning? Because we are never in so great danger as when we have most confidence that we are filled with the Spirit. We are just then most apt to be confident that all our impulses and leading's are Divine leadings, and so we forget to try the spirits whether they be of God. There are men and women who claim to be Spirit filled, and yet are daily doing things that are uncharitable and unrighteous; who apologize for many things that are not only foolish and unwise, but unholy in tendency and selfish in spirit; running to all sorts of fanaticism and folly, perhaps into impurity and iniquity, under the plea that they are guided by the Spirit, until the reality of the Spirit's guidance is brought into contempt. Now observe that this epistle itself puts us on our guard against all this subtle error. It gives us two or three criteria whereby to know the Spirit's leading.

1. He is the Spirit of *obedience*. Chapter 2:2–6. Any spirit
that leads to disobedience, that makes us slaves to fleshly lusts,
the wills of the flesh and of the mind—and the course of this
world—is of the devil.

2. He is the Spirit of *unity.* 4:3, 4. Any spirit that sows seeds
of strife, bitterness, rancors and enmity among disciples, is not
of God.

3. He is the Spirit whose *fruit* is in all goodness, and righteousness, and truth. 5:9. By their fruits ye shall know them.

4. He is the Spirit whose *sword is the Word.* 6:17. And any
guidance which is not through the Scriptures and conformed to
and confirmed by them, is false and delusive.

No other epistle is so emphatic in its presentation of the
danger to be apprehended from hostile and demoniacal principalities and powers, even in the heavenlies. We can never get so
high in our spiritual life that we are beyond the reach of Satanic
wiles and lies, and seductions and suggestions. Nay, it is the
most mature disciple that Satan most surely assaults. While we
are under the sway of fleshly appetites, and of worldly allurements, the Prince of Darkness may safely leave us to our bonds.
But when these bonds are broken and we are enjoying the liberty of sons of God, then we are sure to be the objects of his
malignant assault. It is as in human wars; no general-in-chief
troubles himself about helpless captives; it is the soldier that is
free to fight and strong to overcome, that he watches and seeks
to vanquish and destroy.

If there be any one aim in Ephesians which marks this epistle
as separate from all others, it is found in 3:18, 19. ". . . that we
may be able to comprehend with all saints what is the breadth
and length and depth and height," etc., to measure the immea-
surable dimensions of this sphere of heavenly life, and love, and
privilege. The two prayers of Paul which find record in this

epistle (1:16–23; 3:14–21), find in this their great petition, that the eyes of the heart may be so opened and illumined as that the Ephesian disciples may clearly see and know what is the hope of their calling, and what the riches of the glory of God's inheritance in the saints, and what is the exceeding greatness of His power toward believers; and to know the love of Christ, which passeth knowledge.

As believers we discredit our own privileges and possessions. The statements of the Word of God seem incredible—they pass our comprehension and even apprehension. We can not believe that such things are true. And except the Spirit of God shall open our eyes, illumine our understandings and hearts, and so enable us to know, we shall be blinded by the very glory of our own privileges in Christ, and shall account the whole of this, not only a mystery, but a myth—a poem, a dream. The Holy Spirit alone can make us either to possess or to apprehend what an inheritance we have in God.

The fourfold work of the Spirit is therefore presented in this epistle as nowhere else within the same brief compass: First, *anointing*, which affects the understanding; second, *renewing*, which reaches the disposition; third, *sealing*, which affects the heart and conscience; and fourth, *filling*, which makes speech and conduct full of God. But let us observe that first of all comes that anointing, which makes apprehension of these spiritual truths possible. He must become to us the Spirit of wisdom and revelation in the knowledge of Him before He can make any other of these blessings realities.

Let us then seek to reach to the greatness of this truth. Christ Jesus is essentially a heavenly sphere of life. In Him we are already exalted to the heavenlies. He in heaven as the head imparts to the body an essentially celestial experience, the earnest of the full and final inheritance.

Among these heavenly powers and privileges we may find here suggested even if not expressed:

1. A Heavenly Knowledge of Divine Mysteries.
2. A Heavenly Life or Divine Quickening.
3. A Heavenly Union with Christ and His Saints.
4. A Heavenly Fellowship with all Holy Being.
5. A Heavenly Earnest or Foretaste of Bliss.
6. A Heavenly Access with boldness unto God.
7. A Heavenly Frame, renewed in love.
8. A Heavenly Walk or Conduct, manifest in all the life.
9. A Heavenly Growth to the fullness of stature.
10. A Heavenly Strength and Power to overcome.
11. A Heavenly Assurance or Sealing of the Spirit.
12. A Heavenly Security within the panoply of God.

IV

SUMMARY OF TEACHING IN EPISTLE TO EPHESIANS.

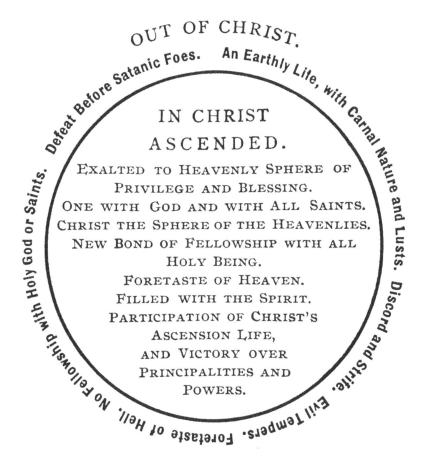

OUT OF CHRIST.

Defeat Before Satanic Foes. An Earthly Life, with Carnal Nature and Lusts. Discord and Strife. Evil Tempers. Foretaste of Hell. No Fellowship with Holy God or Saints.

IN CHRIST ASCENDED.

EXALTED TO HEAVENLY SPHERE OF PRIVILEGE AND BLESSING. ONE WITH GOD AND WITH ALL SAINTS. CHRIST THE SPHERE OF THE HEAVENLIES. NEW BOND OF FELLOWSHIP WITH ALL HOLY BEING. FORETASTE OF HEAVEN. FILLED WITH THE SPIRIT. PARTICIPATION OF CHRIST'S ASCENSION LIFE, AND VICTORY OVER PRINCIPALITIES AND POWERS.

CHAPTER 5

THE EPISTLE TO THE PHILIPPIANS

O bserve how the opening verse salutes all the saints IN *Christ Jesus*, thus bringing to our view this remarkable phrase in the very salutation of the inspired writer—the inscription on the letter. Immediately after, in the eleventh verse, we have the characteristic sentence which again, as a key, unlocks the doors of this epistle: *"Being filled* with the fruits of righteousness which are *by Jesus Christ* unto the glory and praise of God."

This suggests as a ruling thought that in Christ we are full of all the fruits of such abiding, and that no circumstances can destroy our fruitfulness, and, among other fruits, our peace, and rest, and joy in God. This is the divine idea which we meet at every turn. So soon as the writer completes this initial sentence he proceeds to illustrate its truth in his own experience of trial. He records his adverse surroundings, which, were he not in Christ, would be unbearable. He writes as one who is at that time in bonds for Christ (1:13), a prisoner at Rome, and in danger of martyrdom. And yet all this turns to his fuller salvation, and even to the furtherance of the Gospel. His fetters, instead of a restraint, are made to expand and enlarge his service, as part of his privilege to suffer for His sake (1:29), and even to witness for His truth; for, as he was chained in succession to soldiers who were members of the Praetorian guard, he took opportunity thus to spread through the whole Praetorium the good tidings of grace.

In the second chapter he enjoins the Philippians to have in them the same mind as in Christ who "emptied" Himself, and became obedient unto death, even the death of the cross. Then, in chapter 3, the opening exhortation is, "Rejoice in the Lord," while in the third verse one of the three marks of the true circumcision is that we "rejoice in Christ Jesus." This chapter is wholly occupied with the experimental illustration, furnished in Paul's own life, of how a man who is in Christ Jesus finds in Him the *sphere of his perfect satisfaction*. For Christ's sake he had given up and counted as loss whatever he had previously counted as gain; and had made the sacrifice not grudgingly or of necessity, but cheerfully and of choice, because in Christ he had found such full compensation that all else seemed refuse, to be trodden under foot. The world's most precious jewels, the diadems which carnal men most value, seemed to him utterly contemptible beside what he perceived and received in Christ Jesus.

The epistle we are now examining is like one long *song in the night*, a kind of prolonged echo of that midnight prayer and praise which marked Paul's first experience in the city of Philippi when, in answer to the vision of the appeal from Macedonia, he had hastened thither, and got, as his reception, a scourging, a thrusting into an inner prison, and a torturing in the stocks. Yes, the man who sang and prayed in that inner jail is the man who in this epistle, a prisoner at Rome, sings, "Rejoice in the Lord, alway! and again I say, Rejoice!" (Chapter 4:4).

If this epistle has any special keynote which is the controlling thought, in all these melodies of a holy heart, it is this: IN CHRIST JESUS SATISFIED.

If the studious reader of the New Testament would test this for himself, let him take the fourth chapter, for example, and give it a thorough examination. It will be found to contain between the fourth and nineteenth verses at least seven applications and illustrations of that sublime injunction, which so marks not only this chapter, but the whole epistle.

Let us keep before us the grand thought that evidently was the dominant one in the writer's mind, that he who is in Christ Jesus, has entered into *the sphere of complete joy*, where he finds full compensation for all self-denials and sufferings. Without attempting to import any thought into this chapter, but simply to discover what is there, let us note the progress of the Spirit's teaching.

1. If we are in Christ, *He is between us and all our hostile surroundings.* Perhaps, like Paul, we are encompassed by foes and what men call fears, actually prisoners for the Gospel's sake with martyrdom in prospect. What is the Spirit's word to us? "Let your moderation be known unto all men, the Lord is at hand."

We may be permitted to doubt whether even such English words adequately render the brief but sublime original. Let your mildness, gentleness, *forbearingness, το επιεικες*, be manifest to all men—the Lord close by—very near—(εγγυς). This latter expression has been perhaps hastily applied and limited to the Lord's second coming. But may the thought not be even more comforting than this? When, looking at your human environment, you find cause for disquiet, alarm, fear, and are tempted to resistance and self-defense or vindication, God says to you, let your forbearingness be manifest unto all men—remember that the Lord himself is nearer you than anyone else, *between you and your foes.* They can not come within the sphere of your security, nor come between you and Him. Paul himself found that when all men forsook him, the Lord stood by him and strengthened him. And no man perhaps ever lived, whose peace was more absolutely uninterrupted by hostile surroundings, or whose sense of his Master's close proximity proved more absolutely satisfying and sufficient. Are you in Christ Jesus? Remember He is near, very near, next you in respect to interposition, between you and all human foes.

2. If you are in Christ Jesus, you have absolutely *no cause for anxiety.* "Be anxious about nothing, but in everything by prayer and supplication with thanksgiving, let your requests be made known unto God. And the peace of God, which passeth all understanding, shall guard (as a garrison) your hearts and minds through Christ Jesus." (Verses 6 and 7.)

In their way no more striking verses are found in the Word of God. To him who is in Christ Jesus all anxiety is a sin; be anxious for *nothing.* There is a refuge from all fretting care—*in everything* by prayer and supplication. A curious triad! Anxiety for nothing! Thanksgiving for anything! Prayerfulness in everything! And instead of anxious care, peace which passeth understanding—a deep abyss of perplexity and anxiety exchanged for an unfathomable deep of Divine peace—what an exchange! Christ, the sphere of the peace of God, because within that sphere is the God of Peace (verse 9). The sphere of our satisfaction and compensation and consolation is a fortress through which no foe can break—we are literally garrisoned by the peace of God. Be anxious for nothing! He is between you and all care.

Is this an impracticable ideal? Let a simple illustration help us to see how wholly practical and practicable this divine injunction is. There is a vast difference in the *point of view* from which circumstances are regarded. If they come between us and God they may hide God from us; if He comes between us and them, He may hide them from us, or even impart to them, when in themselves alone, they are dark and sad, a lustre and a glory. When the moon comes directly between the earth and the sun it may totally eclipse the orb of day; but when the earth and sun are in another relative position, the moon is at the full, and becomes not an obscurer but a reflector of the sun's light. Our blessed Lord would have us so abide in Him that all care should be shut out, or our very anxieties be transfigured into occasions of thanksgiving.

3. In Christ Jesus you have a *perpetual theme of most exalted thought,* and a perpetual stimulus to holy living, (verses 8, 9). Paul puts before us on the one hand whatsoever things are in themselves virtuous, or inherently desirable; and on the other whatsoever things are of good report, or honorable and influential for good; and he bids us think on these things. And where shall we find more abundant food for such thoughts than in Christ Jesus—the sphere of all excellence? Whatsoever is true, pure, lovely; whatsoever is honest, just, and of good report may be found in Him as nowhere else. And he who is in Christ Jesus, is in the very circle and sphere of such moral and spiritual perfection. All other objects and subjects of thought are shut out by the enamoring vision of His loveliness. When we reflect, moreover, that nothing molds character and conduct like the objects of thought—that to them we are always assimilated, and that the very source and spring of all conduct and even of motive is found in the *thoughts*—it will be readily seen that it is of the highest consequence that we be insphered in Him whose presence makes impossible even the conception of whatever is impure or degrading. Here is the inspiration to exalted and heavenly reflection, meditation, and assimilation. Here we behold as in a glass the glory of the Lord and are changed into

the same image from glory to glory.

4. In Christ Jesus we find *the secret of perfect contentment.* In whatsoever *external state* we are, Christ as our sphere, constitutes our true internal state. Complete in Him, satisfied in Him, all discontent is shut outside such a sphere of life. He is between the believer and all discontent. When tempted to repine and murmur at our lot, we have only to remember that strictly speaking there is no "lot"—no chance in our lives—that everything is arranged, prearranged for our perfecting—we shall be more than content, we shall learn to rejoice and glory in tribulation. We would have our condition just what and only what He wills. Like Pastor Schmolke, with fire sweeping over his parish, death coming into his home, and paralysis and blindness smiting his body, one can still sing,

"My Jesus, as Thou Wilt."

5. In Christ Jesus, the believer finds *strength for all things.* Christ is between him and all weakness; and he can say, "I can do all things in Christ who strengtheneth me." When Paul confronted the thorn in the flesh and besought the Lord thrice that it might depart from him, he learned that great lesson that His grace was sufficient for him; His strength is made perfect in weakness—notice *made perfect*—not only made *manifest.* Had God said to him, "I will reveal my strength in your infirmity," it would have been a great assurance; but, far better than this, only in the weakness of man can God display the *perfection* of His strength. The weaker we are and feel ourselves to be, the stronger He can prove himself to be; so that only when we become perfectly hopeless and helpless in ourselves and absolutely abandon ourselves to Him, can He fully and perfectly glorify His own grace. Omnipotence needs impotence for its sphere of working.

6. In Christ Jesus we learn also a *divine unselfishness, all selfish motives being displaced* by a noble benevolence. This thought is more obscure than some others in this chapter, but like a nugget of gold that a pickax dislodges, it is none the less valuable because it needs a little search to detect it. Twice in this triumphant chapter Paul refers to the bounty of the Philippians. Once before, and again, they had sent to minister to his necessity, and now once more through Epaphroditus. Paul was a prisoner of the Lord, and might be supposed keenly to feel all neglect, and correspondingly appreciate all care for his temporal wants. But, although in that position and condition where temporal needs are greatest and temporal bounties most grateful, we see in this prisoner of the Lord not a trace of *jealousy for himself and his own comfort.* "*Not because I desire a gift, but I desire fruit that may abound to your account.*"

Such unselfishness shines with a sublime light when all the dark, dismal surroundings are taken into consideration. Here is a man who in Christ Jesus has learned to be so content that he is equally happy when he abounds and when he suffers need. When, after an interval of seeming forgetfulness and neglect, the Philippian disciples again sent their gifts to relieve his wants, and comfort his confinement, he "rejoiced," but not at any increase of personal ease, or supply of personal want—no! he rejoiced that now at the last their care of him had again flourished—the word literally means to burst out into leaf and bloom—as a tree in spring. There had been a season during which they seemed barren of unselfish ministries; but now, as in a returning springtime of verdure and blossom, their care of him had burst into beauty; and he rejoiced at their gifts, *as signs of healthy and vigorous life*, or as he says later (verse 18), because this offering to him was a sacrifice acceptable, well pleasing to God, a sweet savor offering; the tree by bursting again into bloom gave forth an odor, a fragrance of sweet smell, that ascended to God! Paul lost all sight of himself in his holy jealousy for their growth in grace, and especially in the consummate grace of giving! Who could learn such unselfishness and self-oblivion save he who in Christ Jesus constantly communed with the One God-man who even on the cross forgot His agonies in the prayer for His murderers, and who was willing to bear the cross and accept such soul-travail as was never known before nor since, if He might bring many souls unto glory?

7. Last of all, in Christ Jesus we find *every need supplied.* Christ is the sphere of God's riches in glory. All want is outside of Him; and all supplies are found in Him.

And so Christ is the sevenfold sphere of the believers' satisfaction. He is between us and all hostile threats, and fears, and foes; between us and all anxieties and cares; between us and all unlovely and harmful thoughts; between us and all murmurs of discontent; between us and all weakness and failure; between us and all selfish absorption in our own advantage; between us and all possible need. Within this sphere of our new life, if our faith be but equal to its perception and reception, we shall find a personal and protecting Presence ever at hand; a perfect peace, passing understanding; everything lovely and of good report for contemplation and assimilation; all strength, Divine strength perfected; all serenity and contentment; all unselfish jealousy for others' growth in grace, and every supply for every need of spirit, soul, and body. What a sphere of satisfaction and exultation!

This epistle especially unfolds to us, and emphasizes for us, that great truth that in Christ Jesus we have a sphere of *perfect peace.*

How much we need it and how far we are from it, in our ordinary experience, no one needs to be told. And yet it is perfectly obvious that all anxiety is both foolish and fatal to all health of body or of mind. It can not avoid or avert any certain evil, while it can crowd the unknown future with imaginary and uncertain calamities and dangers, until we are half insane with the terrors our own imagination has conjured up. Anxiety thus creates false fears, while it makes real calamities doubly hard to bear. Even science and atheistic worldly wisdom says: "Be anxious about nothing."

"Modern science has brought to light the fact that *worry will kill,* and determines, from recent discoveries, how worry kills. Scores of deaths, set down to other causes, are due to worry alone. Anxiety and care, the fretting and chafing of habitual worry, injure beyond repair certain cells of the brain, which being the nutritive center of the body, other organs become gradually injured; and when some disease of these organs, or ailments arise, death finally ensues. Insidiously, worry creeps upon the brain in the form of a single, constant, never-lost idea; and as the dropping of water over a period of years will wear a groove in a stone, so worry, gradually, imperceptibly, but no less surely, destroys the brain cells that are, so to speak, the commanding officers of mental power, health, and motion.

"Worry is an irritant, at certain points, producing little harm if it comes at intervals or irregularly. But against the iteration and reiteration of one idea of a disquieting sort the cells of the brain are not proof. It is as if the skull were laid bare, and the surface of the brain struck lightly with a hammer every few seconds, with mechanical precision, with never a sign of a let-up or the failure of a stroke. Just in this way does the annoying idea, the maddening thought that will not be done away with, strike or fall upon certain nerve cells, never ceasing, and week by week, diminishing the vitality of these delicate organisms, so minute that they can only be seen under the microscope."

Do not worry. Do not hurry. "Let your moderation be

known to all men." Court the fresh air day and night. Sleep and rest abundantly. Sleep is nature's benediction. Spend less nervous energy each day than you make. Be cheerful. "A light heart lives long." Think only healthful thoughts. "As a man thinketh in his heart, so he is." "Seek peace and pursue it." Avoid passion and excitement. Associate with healthy people. Health is contagious as well as disease. Don't carry the whole world on your shoulders, far less the universe. "Trust in God and do the right." Never despair. "Lost hope is a fatal disease." "If ye know these things happy are ye if ye do them."

If such be the voice of worldly wisdom, let us listen to the wisdom that is from above. And remember the sublime saying of the sainted George Müller. When his helpers were asked how they could account for the fact that his serene calm was undisturbed when, with two thousand orphans to clothe and feed, there was neither food in the larder nor money in the bank, and his one resort was prayer—the answer was, that it could be accounted for only on his own philosophy:

> Where anxiety begins, faith ends;
> And where faith begins, anxiety ends.

V

SUMMARY OF TEACHING IN EPISTLE TO THE PHILIPPIANS.

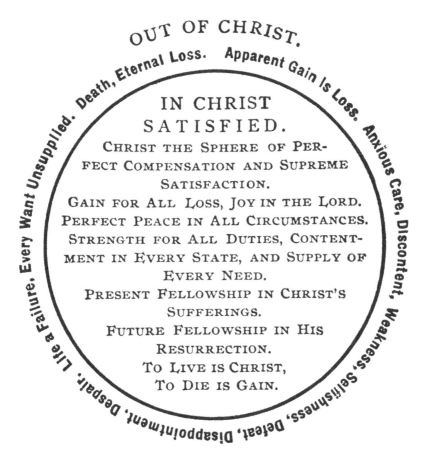

OUT OF CHRIST.

Death, Eternal Loss.   Apparent Gain Is Loss.

Every Want Unsupplied.   Anxious Care, Discontent, Weakness,

Life a Failure,   Selfishness, Defeat, Disappointment, Despair.

IN CHRIST SATISFIED.

CHRIST THE SPHERE OF PERFECT COMPENSATION AND SUPREME SATISFACTION.

GAIN FOR ALL LOSS, JOY IN THE LORD.

PERFECT PEACE IN ALL CIRCUMSTANCES.

STRENGTH FOR ALL DUTIES, CONTENTMENT IN EVERY STATE, AND SUPPLY OF EVERY NEED.

PRESENT FELLOWSHIP IN CHRIST'S SUFFERINGS.

FUTURE FELLOWSHIP IN HIS RESURRECTION.

TO LIVE IS CHRIST, TO DIE IS GAIN.

CHAPTER 6

THE EPISTLE TO THE COLOSSIANS

In Colossians again we meet the phrase, in Christ Jesus, in the very salutation, 1:2. And in the prayer that immediately follows, that ye might be filled with the knowledge of His will, etc. *(πληρωθητε.)*

Here we first strike the great word of this epistle, which is *πληρωμα*—an untranslatable word.

The substance of the teaching of Colossians is this: In Christ Jesus we have the pleroma of God. This idea is inwrought into the structure of the epistle and curiously into its language.[1]

The idea is that all this divine fullness dwells in Him, and may dwell in us by our dwelling in Him.

This introduces us to the *Power* and *Perfection* of *Christ, as the sphere of our New Life:* IN HIM, COMPLETE.

Here, as in Ephesians, there are ten blessings that are already ours, and one that is to be ours at His coming. And it is curious to compare the *ten* things of Ephesians, with those of this epistle:

---

1 We meet here and there words into which the root πληρόω enters: πληρωθητε, 1:9. παν το πληρωμα, 1:19, 2:9. ανταναπληρω, 1:24. πληρωσαι, to fulfil the word, 1:25. πληροφοριας, 2:2, full assurance. πεπληρωμενοι. 10, complete. πεπληροφορημενοι, 4:12, complete in full measure.

EPHESIANS	COLOSSIANS
CHOSEN	ROOTED
PREDESTINATED	BUILT UP
ACCEPTED	ESTABLISHED
REDEEMED	FILLED FULL
FORGIVEN	CIRCUMCISED
QUICKENED*	BURIED
RAISED*	QUICKENED*
SEATED*	RISEN*
SEALED	SEATED*
OBTAINED INHERITANCE	HID
TO BE GATHERED IN ONE	TO BE MANIFESTED

Three in both lists are alike (which we mark with an asterisk), all the rest are unlike; but in Ephesians the list has reference to oneness of saints in Christ and the present privilege of life in Him; in Colossians, to the completeness of all and every believer in Him, and the perfection and power which are realized in Christ.

Hence the same figure in both epistles: Christ the Head of Body; there with reference to *unity*, and here, to *vitality*. The ruling thought then in this epistle is found in the fullness of Christ, as the sphere of our life. (He is filled with God, and in Him we also are filled with God. In fact the word, *pleroma*, as already remarked, can not be translated. It means more than fullness. It is a term used by philosophy, and borrowed by Paul from philosophic authors. They claimed to know the secret of something that filled up all human deficiency—a plenitude of knowledge and power. Paul claims that in Christ the true pleroma is found: that He as the Son of God has all the plenitude of the godhead in Him, in full measure, and running over—and so, if we are in Him, all that Divine pleroma becomes ours. Whatever perfection is in God, in His knowledge, power, strength, wisdom, love, holiness, thus fills up to the full our measure of capacity.

In the light of this truth the whole epistle becomes luminous. 1:27. Paul speaks of the riches of the glory of this mystery—which is Christ in you, the hope of glory; and in Verse 28: That we may present every man perfect in Christ Jesus.

Again in 1:19. It pleased the Father that in Him should all the pleroma dwell.

2:3. In Whom are hid all the treasures of wisdom and knowledge.

2:6, 7. As ye have received Christ Jesus the Lord, so walk in Him, rooted and built up in Him and stablished in the faith.

Note particularly verses 8, 9, etc., as the heart of the epistle. He warns against philosophy, which holds out its false pleroma, and says: In Him dwelleth all the pleroma of the godhead bodily, and ye have the pleroma in Him.

If the word pleroma is untranslatable, what shall we say of the *thought* of the epistle! What words shall adequately translate such a conception into human language, or convey it to human minds! It is the same essential idea as that which seeks expression in that last and greatest parable ever spoken by our Lord: The vine and the branches. There several words form the salient points of thought, arresting attention: Vine, branch, and fruit; *abide,* ask; love, joy. The grand word of the seven is ABIDE, and the grand lesson is absolute and perpetual dependence on the one hand, and perfect and perpetual fullness of blessing on the other. Let us remember that in the vine dwells all vegetable fullness, all the fullness of soil and sap, of life and strength; and that the branch abides in the vine that it may be filled with all the fullness of the vine. Branch life, like limb life in the body, can never become independent. The child may outgrow the mother's care, and support and nourish the parent; but the branch can never outgrow its dependence, nor can the limb ever become independent of the body. The same in nature and nurture, in root and soil and sap, in life and growth, the very leaves, blooms, clusters of the branch are the leaves, blooms, and clusters of the vine. It is the full life of the vine, pushing its way through the branch's channels, that exhibits itself in every new twig, bud, flower, grape; and, as the grape rounds out into luscious fullness, it is the vine which imparts its own fullness in the juice and color and perfection of the cluster. The disciple abides in Christ, and so his asking becomes Christ's asking; his love and joy are in fact Christ's love and joy abiding in him and filling him. So what in the parable is suggested or enfolded, is, in this epistle, unfolded. In Him dwelleth all the fullness of the godhead bodily and substantially, and we are filled full in Him of the same pleroma of God. The thought is inexpressible. Even the Holy Ghost finds no intelligible terms to convey it; all attempts are like groanings unutterable.

The ten or eleven specific statements of what the disciple has in Christ, all have reference to this pleroma or fullness of power and perfection. We are rooted in Him—and so like a plant we have fullness of strength and life—so well expressed by the roots which take fast hold on the soil and absorb whatever promotes growth and strength.

We are built up in Him—like the building which gets stability from its rock foundation, and beauty and completeness as carried on to completion.

When we are taught that in Him we are circumcised, buried, made alive, risen, seated, hid in God, and to be manifested when He is—one of the greatest thoughts of the Word is put before us. Christ is the great *Representative Man*—the second and Last Adam, the Son of Man. All that He experienced, from His miraculous conception to His session at God's right hand, is representative—that is, it is in our behalf, typical as well as historical, and we are to look upon ourselves as going through all these experiences in Him. When Adam was on trial, the whole race he represented was on trial, and his fall was representative. When Christ was on trial, it was a representative of the race—the Last Adam—who was tempted, and triumphed. God in Christ sees us, who believe, victorious over the devil and Death, the world and the flesh. It is a great mystery of Grace; but in Him we were circumcised, and put away fleshly lusts—in Him buried, that the old corrupt nature might be left in the tomb, and in Him by the Holy Ghost we were made alive unto God, raised to live a new life, by His power lifted to the heavenly sphere of life; so that now our real life is not that which is seen. It is a *hidden* life. The world knows us not, because it knew Him not. The springs of our true life are in Him, and in heaven. This thought is not capable of conveyance by human language or illustration. Zechariah seeks to forecast it in the vision of the Golden Candlestick, whose lamps are fed through golden pipes from the two living olive trees. Every disciple is united to Christ by unseen channels, and the life we live is by the faith of the Son of God—as the branch receives life from the vine, or the plant from the sun and air of heaven. Every day of holy living is a day of living contact with the invisible world and the unseen God—Heaven's power communicated to earthly beings. And not until Christ is manifested, coming out of His long hiding beside the Father, will this hidden life of ours appear. When He is manifested in glory with His resurrection body, and ours is made like unto His and we are seen bearing His perfect likeness, it will be seen that all this is absolutely true; as He is, so are we in this world.

Christ came to do God's will, and took in His incarnation a body prepared for Him, and in a higher sense, another body—the Church—after His resurrection. This body is thus seated

with Him in the heavenlies, and all enemies are to become the
footstool of Christ and His mystical body, bruised, under His
feet. We have a right in Him to this exalted seat in the heavenlies, and to sit down with Him in peace, as those who have the
sense of a finished work and completed conquest, henceforth
in Him expecting—anticipating, that all foes will be made our
footstool. So far as we can take this in by faith, they are already
subdued. He says, to every believer who can receive it, "'Stretch
forth thy withered hand!' and henceforth to find restored facul-
ties for holy work; 'Rise, take up thy bed, thou paralytic!' henceforth to find power to walk with God; 'Woman, thou art loosed
from thine infirmity!' henceforth be erect and upright and no
longer bowed down and bent into deformity by Satan."

The greatest difficulty today among us believers is that we
have no true apprehension of the actual present fullness, the
pleroma of divine power, wisdom, strength, victory, which is in
God for us, and may be found in Christ, as the sphere of our
full life and energy. *There* is the secret of all failure: we do not
avail ourselves of this fullness of God. We do not practically
believe our high calling, nor perceive the riches of the glory of
God's inheritance in the saints, and consequently the exceeding
greatness of His power to usward who believe—the standard of
which is the working of that omnipotence in Christ, when God
raised Him from the dead and seated Him at His own right
hand in the heavenlies. Oh, the unclaimed riches of the believer
in Christ Jesus!

This pleroma may be viewed in two aspects, and is so presented in this epistle: The completeness in Christ, first, as my
representative before God; and, secondly, as God's representative before me.

It must be remembered that He is both the Son of Man and
the Son of God, and perfect in both relations.

It is a curious fact, showing the marvelous completeness also of the teaching whereby this truth is presented, that there are but two cases in this epistle where this word, pleroma, recurs, and they mark the divisions of thought we are now considering. Chapter 1:19. It pleased the Father that in Him should all fullness dwell. This is spoken of Him as *Head of the body, the Church*, which is a human institution, composed of redeemed sons of men. Chapter 2:9. For in Him dwelleth all the fullness of the godhead bodily. Here the statement is made as to His relation to the godhead, not manhood.

In Him we are circumcised, buried, risen, seated at God's right hand; that is said of Him as my representative; what is true of the Head of the body, is true of the body whose head He is.

But, when we are told that in Him we have redemption, that by Him God reconciles all things to Himself; that in Him are hid all the treasures of wisdom and knowledge, it is manifest that the fullness of God toward us is meant.

These two thoughts may find an imperfect illustration in an advocate at court. Let us suppose a very difficult case at law, but on which everything hangs, property, reputation, character, life. I secure the services of the most competent and eminent of lawyers. Now, what does he do? First, he represents my case before the court, but he also represents the court before me. He could not take my case in charge if he did not understand my case perfectly, nor could he if he did not understand the law perfectly. Christ is my advocate before God, for He is the Son of Man and understands *me;* He is the Son of God and understands HIM; and being perfect in both relations, He becomes my Mediator; in Him I have a perfect representative godward, and God has a perfect representative manward.

The practical bearing of this double truth is immense; a whole lifetime will give us but a glimpse of the infinite value of such a Savior. As son of man everything about His human character and life has reference to the believer. As He is, so are we in this world. Because I believe in Him, and am united to Him, all His experiences become my own. His sinless perfection, His divine patience, His holy obedience, His triumph over Satan, are imputed to me: in Him I am presented as perfect before God. But, as Son of God, whatever He is to me, God is. I am to know the mind and heart and disposition of God toward me by knowing Christ's attitude toward me, because as He is, so is God in Heaven. Hence He said to Philip: "Have I been so long time with you, and yet hast thou not known Me, Philip? He that hath seen Me, hath seen the Father; and how sayest thou then, Show us the Father?"

In this Epistle to the Colossians we reach almost the climax of the Scripture teaching about the second and last Adam. Four or five passages need to be carefully studied by those who would take in the full meaning of this wonderful teaching: Psalm 8, compared with Hebrews 2:6–18; Romans 5:12–21; 1 Corinthians 15:21–28; and 45–49; and the Epistles to the Ephesians and the Colossians. In the Epistle to the Romans, Adam is the figure of the Coming One. 5:14. In 1 Corinthians, He is the Lord of resurrection life and victory. In the Epistles to the Ephesians and Colossians, He is the representative of the believer in His whole human and heavenly experience. He stands in his stead, and in His own miraculous birth, circumcision, baptism, temptation, crucifixion, burial, resurrection, ascension, session at God's right hand, and coming again, the believer may see, set forth, his own regeneration, separation unto God, confession of faith, conquest over Satan, satisfaction of legal penalty, life in the Spirit, exaltation to heavenly privilege, and inheritance of final glory.

This prepares for the absolute climax of this teaching in

Hebrews 2, where we see Jesus Christ, finally exalted to universal dominion, and, *in Him*, the redeemed Adamic race once more raised to the throne and scepter. The Eighth Psalm is not to be fulfilled in the first Adam, whose fall wrecked all his prospects of sovereignty, until the second Adam restores the ruins of the first, and gives lost man his true seat at God's right hand.

VI

Summary of Teaching in Epistle to the Colossians.

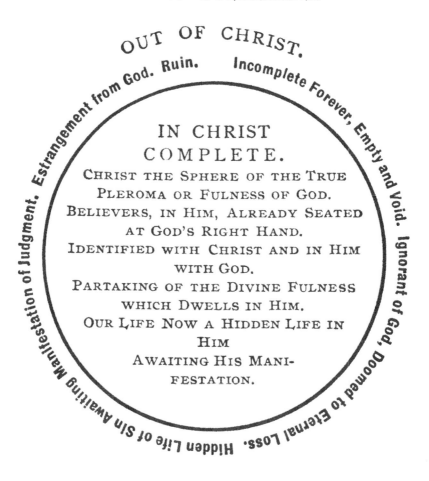

OUT OF CHRIST.

Estrangement from God. Ruin.   Incomplete Forever, Empty and Void. Ignorant of God. Doomed to Eternal Loss. Hidden Life of Sin Awaiting Manifestation of Judgment.

IN CHRIST COMPLETE.

CHRIST THE SPHERE OF THE TRUE PLEROMA OR FULNESS OF GOD. BELIEVERS, IN HIM, ALREADY SEATED AT GOD'S RIGHT HAND. IDENTIFIED WITH CHRIST AND IN HIM WITH GOD. PARTAKING OF THE DIVINE FULNESS WHICH DWELLS IN HIM. OUR LIFE NOW A HIDDEN LIFE IN HIM AWAITING HIS MANIFESTATION.

CHAPTER 7

THE EPISTLES TO THE THESSALONIANS

The keynote of both of these letters is promptly struck in the third verse of the first chapter, in the phrase, *patience of hope in our Lord Jesus Christ*. Here we are turned toward the future, the second coming of Him in Whom we find the *sphere of our final triumph over all foes*. Hope looks forward to the future and fixes its gaze on this consummation, and hence becomes the profound secret of *patience* in present trials. The same blessed thought reappears in verses 9, 10. *"To serve* the living God, and *to wait* for His Son from heaven."

These two epistles therefore carry us to the climax of the glorious truth which has lifted us to higher and higher elevations, as we have gone from summit to summit in studying this progress of doctrine; here the Holy Spirit gives us a glimpse of our final, ultimate, and complete victory in Christ over all enemies and all trials.

It will be remembered that, in the Epistles to the Ephesians and the Colossians, we found one blessed privilege to lie in the future: in the former, our gathering together unto Him; and in the latter, our manifestation in Him. Here we are emphatically reminded of His reappearing, at which time this gathering together of all saints is to take place about the very Head of the mystical body; and their manifestation in Him, because He himself is to be manifested in glory.

The Holy Spirit guides the pen of Paul to write of these two future and crowning relations of blessing that yet await all God's saints. Compare 2 Thessalonians 2:1, 8. "By our gathering together unto Him," and, "the brightness of His coming"—the epiphany of His Parousia. Here we have both thoughts; and in fact both are found in the one verse which opens second chapter: "Now we beseech you, brethren, by *the coming of our Lord Jesus Christ,* and *by our gathering together unto Him.*"

To get even a glimpse of this truth, we must first know *what is included* in this second advent of the Son of God, as it is set forth in these two letters to Thessalonica. We present the following as a partial analysis of their contents, but sufficient to hint at the wealth of suggestion herein to be discovered:

1. The reward of service. 1 Thessalonians 2:19. For what is our hope, or joy, or crown of rejoicing? Are not even ye in the presence of our Lord Jesus Christ at His coming?

2. The final perfection in holiness. 1 Thessalonians 3:13. Unblamable in holiness at the coming, etc.

3. The reunion of departed and surviving saints. 1 Thessalonians 4:13–18.

4. The triumph over death in the resurrection of the dead and the translation and transformation of the living. 1 Thessalonians 4:16, 17.

5. The final consummation of salvation. Living together with Him, forevermore. 1 Thessalonians 4:17.

6. The avenging of saints upon all adversaries. 1 Thessalonians 5:9; 2 Thessalonians 1:7–10.

7. The ultimate gathering together unto Him. 2 Thessalonians 2:1.

8. The destruction of the man of sin. 2 Thessalonians 2:8.

9. The obtaining of the glory of our Lord Jesus Christ. 2 Thessalonians 2:14.

10. The final, eternal glorification of saints in Him. 2 Thessalonians 2:16.

When Christ comes again to complete our salvation, there will be at least a fourfold triumph:

1. Over sin, in unblamable holiness.

2. Over suffering, endured at the hands of the wicked.

3. Over death, in resurrection and translation.

4. Over Antichrist and the devil.

And in this triumph the saints are to be in every respect *copartakers with Christ.* His triumph is theirs, and His joy is theirs.

Only in this grand consummation will it be possible to understand what it is to be *in Christ Jesus.* In our present experience several necessary hindrances exist to our full realization of the blessedness of our estate in Him.

1. First, All this sphere pertains to the *invisible.* We as yet belong to a material and temporal order. Things visible and sensible appeal to us, because our physical senses are on the alert to receive impression. We walk by sight naturally and inevitably; and the unseen and eternal can be apprehended and appreciated only in part, dimly, even by those whose inner spiritual senses are exercised to discern good and evil. To see the visible we need only to open our natural eyes—it is easier to keep them open than shut, and to walk by sight requires no effort. But to see the invisible and feel the power of the eternal, is not natural nor easy; it requires sedulous and constant effort—the daily discipline of our higher senses. These things evade and escape us if we are careless, nay, unless we are most prayerful and careful; and at times the most devout and circumspect believer loses the vision

of their entrancing loveliness, preciousness, and glory, and sets his eye on the lower good that seems so much easier both to see and grasp. But when Christ comes again and is manifested, He will be *revealed*, and all our being will be filled with the enamoring *sense* of his reality, and we shall never *lose sight* of Him more. The now unseen and eternal will then be as vividly real as any objects of sight or sense.

2. Secondly, This sphere of our life in Christ is now of necessity *partial*. We are *in* this world, however little we may be *of* it, and we can not escape more or less of its *contact*, however free from its *contamination*. Our enjoyment of Christ is interrupted by earthly and carnal surroundings, even when the lower cravings are subdued. From time to time we are recalled to a painful sense of the fact that *sin* is in us, however free we may be from *sins* and *sinning*. We are compassed about with infirmity of body, mind, and will; and the thorn in the flesh can not be wholly forgotten even in the all-sufficient grace. The weakness is there, even while the strength is made perfect, for that is the condition of its perfect exhibition and manifestation. Perhaps it is not too much to say that perfect enjoyment of God is impossible, for our condition and character are yet imperfect or unperfect. How different when the last bond is broken, the last tie severed, and we are free to be *only in Christ*, not even the *body* longer hindering our perfect resemblance to Him and perfect communion with Him! What approximation to perfection may be possible, probably no saint has yet known or shown; doubtless greater measures of resemblance to Him and more complete absorption in Him are possible and practicable than any saint has ever yet experienced; but it is plain that we must wait until He comes, and we meet Him face to face, and with bodies fashioned like unto His, ourselves without blemish, as He is, before our inspherement in Him can reach its completeness.

3. Thirdly, Our sphere of life in Christ is now *contested*. We are in the midst of adversaries, and sometimes their presence is more vividly and awfully real to us than that of our Advocate. Without are fightings, within are fears. However secure in Christ, we feel the danger to be constant and imminent. The five foes of whom we have found the Holy Spirit reminding us, are not slain, nor are they, to our experience, routed. They reappear with such frequency that we are never wholly free from their taunting, torturing presence. What saint, from Paul to Müller, has ever entirely found conscious liberty from the law in grace! How we need to keep reminding ourselves that we are on Sion, not under Sinai! How perpetually are we shadowed by the sense of condemnation! Who has ever entirely escaped the allurements of the world, so that he is actually dead to its censure or approval, indifferent to its opposition or cooperation, insensible to its attractions and its ridicule? Who is there who is never worldly-minded and finds no need of a new turning of the mirror of the mind from the lower to the higher realm?

Has any saint ever found the flesh and the carnal man subdued? The very fact that every one of us finds the flesh lusting against the Spirit, and the Spirit contending against the flesh, and that we feel these to be contrary, one to the other, so that we *may not*, according to the Spirit, do the things that we would, according to the flesh, shows how to the last we have to acknowledge our deliverance to be but partial.

Need it be said that the self-life is *never* wholly destroyed in us while we are in the world? We may think that self is dead, but our very *thought* is an evidence of its survival, and perhaps a proof of its pride. We slay self in one form, and it seems to be the more alive in every other, until what we think the death of self-praise, proves only the boastfulness of a conscious humility which is proven, by such consciousness, to be no humility at all.

Here is the subtlest of our foes, and the most persistent of life, as well as the most multiplied of form.

And as to the devil, obviously he is not dead. The saintliest priest of God can not stand at His altar without the unseen Satanic foe at his right hand to resist him. We go up to the heavenlies in the rapt communion with God, but *in the heavenlies* are the hostile principalities and powers (Ephesians 6:10). There is no escape from the approach of this devouring lion. We may indeed escape his jaws and his paws, but we hear his roar and we tremble as we remember how many in their securest moments have become his victims.

The day will come, when even Death, the last enemy, will be destroyed, and we shall be free to enjoy Him who is our life, without even the presence of a foe. What a life that will be in Him—when the law is forever silenced as our accuser, and Sinai's summit forever disappears! What a freedom when sin no longer dwells in us, but our very nature is purged of its hateful presence! What a deliverance, when the world to come displaces the world that now is, and there are no allurements that draw from God! What a death, when self gives up the ghost, and the life of Christ is all the life we know! When the flesh and carnal mind are eternally gone, that the Spirit may rule every motion within us! And, when the bottomless pit closes its doors over the adversary of God and man, never again to release him; and, before the Lion of the tribe of Judah, the lion that roars in our path and seeks to devour our souls, falls in final destruction— what a shout of deliverance will ring through all the universe of redeemed souls and unfallen angels!

Over these two epistles might be written one sublime word, *victory.* A salvation complete and glorious draws nearer than when we believed, and this is held up before us continually in these two letters. The phrases which abound here are found in their variety and combination nowhere else, for they grow naturally out of such a soil: "patience of hope," "joy of the Holy Ghost," "to wait for His Son from heaven," "God who hath called you unto His kingdom and glory," "at the coming of our Lord Jesus Christ with all His saints," "the Lord Jesus shall be revealed from heaven," etc. And, as these phrases abound, so these epistles abound in arguments for holy living drawn from the glorious and blessed hope which illumines the future. There is scarce a grace or virtue in the whole blessed catalogue of saintly excellencies and adornments, for which this future victory and glory presents no new incentive; obedience, service, patience, fidelity, self-denial, love, meditation on the Word, joy, comfort, steadfastness, zeal, sanctity, honesty, hope, consolation, vigilance, humility, gentleness, supplication, separation to God, peace—all that is most lovely and most helpful is made to hang upon the cherishing of the blessed assurance of our final triumph and blessedness, in Him who is the Coming One. Only so far as this blessed hope is obscured or practically becomes inoperative in our lives, will our character and conduct as disciples degenerate.

Let us remember that the coming of our Lord Jesus Christ is the consummation of all things which pertain to our redemption. It introduces the sublime closing scenes in the whole history of salvation. There is much that can not be revealed to the Church and to the angelic host in the age that now is, and God waits for the ages to come to make known His manifold wisdom and grace. He finds in our present experience no *data* from which to convey a fit knowledge—no *dialect* sufficiently meaningful to express the inexpressible things which must wait for the revelation of experience.

The more devoutly we study the Word, the more we shall discover that, like our Lord's first advent, the present revelation of grace is a necessary hiding of God's true power; new conditions are necessary for a full disclosure. When He comes again He will not come in disguise, but in proper attire and with proper attendance. He will be *revealed* as never before. And all spiritual truth and fact, pertaining to the believer, waits for His true epiphany, when His glory shall emerge out of clouds into fullness of revelation. We can only, like the Thessalonians, *"serve and wait."* To the most mature saint, that coming day is to be as absolute a surprise as the third heaven mysteries were to Paul. God has something beyond all we have conceived, waiting for us, at Christ's appearing. The words used to intimate it are the best human language supplies, but the mold is too small for the conception, and so cramps it and so distorts it. We must *see* in order to *know*, and for that vision we wait, with longing and expectant eyes, until the dazzling splendor of the coming King shall declare what no words can reveal or unveil.

VII

Summary of Teaching in Epistle to the Thessalonians.

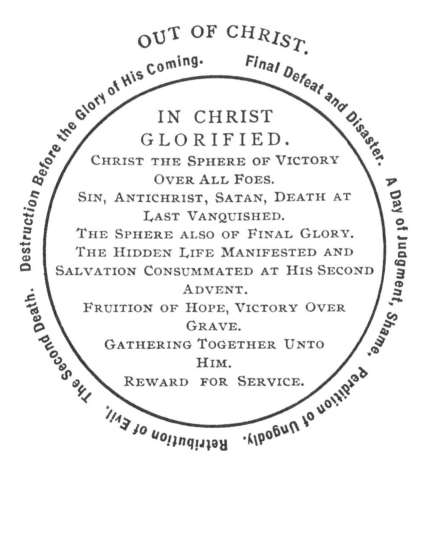

OUT OF CHRIST.

Final Defeat and Disaster.

Before the Glory of His Coming.

Destruction

A Day of Judgment, Shame,

Perdition of Ungodly.

Retribution of Evil.

The Second Death.

IN CHRIST
GLORIFIED.
CHRIST THE SPHERE OF VICTORY
OVER ALL FOES.
SIN, ANTICHRIST, SATAN, DEATH AT
LAST VANQUISHED.
THE SPHERE ALSO OF FINAL GLORY.
THE HIDDEN LIFE MANIFESTED AND
SALVATION CONSUMMATED AT HIS SECOND
ADVENT.
FRUITION OF HOPE, VICTORY OVER
GRAVE.
GATHERING TOGETHER UNTO
HIM.
REWARD FOR SERVICE.

CHAPTER 8

CONCLUSION

As we review our studies of this sevenfold group of letters to the early Christian disciples, we find, first, a very remarkable *completeness of presentation* of this great privilege of the believer. He is IN CHRIST JESUS. In Him, he finds a new *sphere of life* with sevenfold blessing. First, *justification* with its new standing and acceptance before God. Second, *sanctification* with its new power for holy living in the Spirit of God. Third, *fellowship* with God in the actual practical walk in newness of life. Fourth, *exaltation* to the heavenlies in an earnest or foretaste of a heavenly life. Fifth, *compensation* for all present self-denials and sufferings and renunciations for Christ's sake. Sixth, *identification* with Christ in His present hidden life at the right hand of the Father. Seventh, *glorification* when He comes to be admired and adored of all His waiting body, the members, whose manifestation awaits His final epiphany as their head. To this scarce anything could be added. All that subsequent epistles can do is to amplify what is here suggested.

We notice also a marked *progress of thought* which is the more remarkable inasmuch as the *canonical* order of the books we have studied is not their *chronological* and *historical* order.

As to the composition of these letters, First Thessalonians, one of the last, belongs first. We might almost say the canonical order *reverses* the historical. And yet the order of the teaching, as we have seen, is exactly correspondent to the *order of events* in our Lord's human life, so that we can not imagine these epistles to have fallen by accident into their existing arrangement any more than "a dropped alphabet could be picked up, an Iliad," or fragments of many-colored glass could be thrown together into a mosaic. Behind the order of these books, as they appear in our New Testament, must lie a guiding Hand.

Manifestly there are, in our Lord's human and mediatorial life, seven marked stages, which naturally associate themselves with certain events whose order is unchangeable:

1. His death, burial, and resurrection.

2. His breathing of the indwelling Spirit into His disciples.

3. His forty days of walk in resurrection newness of life.

4. His ascension to the heavenlies and gift of the Spirit in power.

5. His compensation for suffering in the joy set before Him.

6. His session at the right hand of God—the hidden life above.

7. His manifestation or final epiphany in His second advent.

But this is exactly, and in every particular, the order of thought as found in these epistles, which, as we have said, are *not* in the order of their production by the inspired writer.

In the Epistle to the Romans the death, burial, and resurrection of our Lord are the center of the argument, and are specially conspicuous.

In the two Epistles to the Corinthians, the grand controlling, pervading conception is that of the Holy Spirit, as the very breath of God, imparted to disciples, and becoming in them the secret of holiness.

In the Epistle to the Galatians the emphasis is upon the walk in the Spirit, wherein the lusts of the flesh are no longer fulfilled, and new liberty is found for service.

In the Epistle to the Ephesians we are taught that, in Christ, we are ascended into the heavenlies and, while living on earth, essentially experience heavenly joys. Notice here also the emphasis upon the Pentecostal gift of the Spirit, as the Spirit of Love and Power.

In the Epistle to the Philippians, the great thought is the joy set before us, which makes all the best things of earth to seem mere refuse and dross, to be trodden under foot; and all partaking of Christ's sufferings, nothing but an occasion of rejoicing.

In the Epistle to the Colossians, we see our privilege of being, in Christ, seated at God's right hand, so that we reckon on all future victories over sin as already accomplished.

In the Epistles to the Thessalonians our ultimate participation with our ascended Lord in the glory of His reappearing and the final triumph over death and the grave, are set before us.

It might be observed that this order is conspicuously similar to that in the Intercessory Prayer in John 17, where we are led on from the *sanctity*, or separation unto God, of the believers, to their *unity* with Christ and each other, and then to their final beholding and sharing of His *glory*.

The present schemes for church unity too often overlook the fact that the basis for all true unity must be found, not in a new *organization* more compact in character, but a *new sanctification*, more complete in its nature. The Epistle to the Ephesians first, of all the epistles, unfolds *the oneness of believers* in Christ Jesus. Paul ascribes to Him the making one of both Jew and Gentile, and the breaking down of the middle wall of partition—that balustrade of stone separating the court of the Gentiles from the Holy Place, beyond which it was death for any Gentile to pass. And there was a further "middle wall of partition," which excluded even Jews from the court of priests, and from the Holiest of All. Ephesians 2:14.

That epistle, which also in the fourth chapter gives the septiform of Christian unity, teaches us that it is a *unity of the Spirit*, and only as that Spirit of God is in actual control, can there be a true inward unity. Such unity as Christ prayed for is dependent on sanctity, and prepares for glory. Let us be content with no other—unification is not always unity.

The companion thought to all this is one which ministers to our highest consolation and comfort: "Herein is our love made perfect that we may have boldness in the Day of Judgment, because, as He is, so are we in this world." 1 John 4:17. The only way for Love to be made perfect, so as to cast out fear, and so that we may have boldness in the Day of Judgment, is to remember and realize our *complete oneness with* Him—*that, as He is there, so are we here;* all that He is and has attained, obtained, secured, by His atoning death and holy obedience and mediation, He is and has, as our representative—the second Adam.

Neither the Day of Judgment nor the day of reward is wholly future. Every day is one of award. Whenever we confront the Word of God, His Holy Spirit, His law, our own conscience, the all-knowing God himself, we are in the virtual presence of His mercy seat and judgment seat. And in the midst of all the terrors of His omniscient eye, there is but one deliverance from mortal fear—*we are in Christ* and identified with Him. God sees us not as we are in ourselves, but as we are in Christ Jesus; and condemnation is impossible, as impossible to us as to Him. And so, wonderful as it seems, because we are in Him, His reward is ours, and to realize in any measure our oneness with Him is so far to anticipate and make present in foretaste our day of coronation and glorification. Our one aim should therefore be a full *appropriation by* us of all that is freely given *to* us, and appropriated by God *for* us in our Lord Jesus. We should seek to cast out unbelief, and in faith receive and enjoy all that our God has bestowed and challenged us to claim as our own, in Him.

The study of this subject, as thus unfolded in these epistles, is *A study of salvation.* This word is used in the New Testament in at least *three* very distinct and yet associated senses:

1. Of an *accomplished fact.* Luke 19:9. "This day is salvation come to this house."

2. Of a *process to be carried on* through life. Philippians 2:12. "Work out your own salvation," κατεργάζεσθε, work out thoroughly, carry to completion.

3. Of a *final result in perfection* in glory. 1 Peter 1:5. "Kept by the power of God through faith unto salvation, ready to be revealed in the last day," αποκαλυφθηναι, to be brought to light as something hitherto hidden.

It is worthy of particular notice that the *first* and *last* are simply bestowed by grace as a gift of God, not of ourselves or having any direct connection with our endeavors or cooperation. But the *second* depends upon our joint action with God. "Work out your own salvation, for it is God who worketh in you both to will and to work." All through, the salvation is wholly a divine work; but it is beautiful to observe how clearly defined in each case, and how distinct, our attitude is. When salvation comes to us as to Zaccheus, our attitude is simply that of the *faith* which receives, accepts, appropriates the gift of God. The salvation, which we work out with fear and trembling, demands a *love* responsive to God's love, and which yields our will to His will, and leads us to work as He works in us. The salvation which He reserves for us and reveals at the final advent of our Lord in glory, is one upon which our *hope* is to fix its gaze and which it is to hold in perpetual contemplation.

Taken together these three give us the *complete conception of salvation*. It begins in *justification*, which is received at once and forever as the free gift of God by faith in Christ. The process of salvation is *sanctification*, in which our new love to God leads us to will what He wills, and work out what He works in. The completed and glorious salvation, which awaits us at the last day, is our *glorification*, which our hope is to anticipate and contemplate as a final state of perfection.

A comprehensive presentation of the *whole* matter may be found in Titus 2:11–13, which is a very conspicuous statement of the entire work of Christ in human salvation. Here are two appearings or epiphanies of our Lord. At the first, there is a salvation brought to all men; at the second, a salvation perfected in glory for saints; and, between the two, there lies the experience of the disciple in this present evil age, when he is to work out his own salvation—by denying himself ungodliness and every worldly lust, and by living soberly (as to himself), righteously (as to other men), and godly (as to God).

No man has any proper sense of the grandeur of Christ's work of salvation, who does not apprehend the threefold aspect of that work; and much confusion of ideas will be avoided so soon as we get these distinctions clearly fixed in mind.

For example, how much needless mystification has come from not properly understanding the *two apparent conditions* of salvation in Paul's famous "word" or message "of faith" in Romans 10:8, 9, 10. Here inquirers after salvation have often stumbled, because confession with the mouth seems coupled with belief in the heart, as though the two were equally necessary to salvation; whereas, in no other case is confession thus made essential. For example, Philip told the eunuch, Acts 8:37: "If thou believest with all thine heart thou mayest." And Paul told the Philippian jailer (Acts 16:30, 31): "Believe on the Lord Jesus Christ and thou shalt be saved." There is no mistaking New Testament teaching on this point. See Acts 13:38, 39, where Paul in the synagogue at Antioch in Pisidia says: "By Him all that believe are justified from all things."

How then can this same Paul teach Roman Christians that confession with the mouth is essential to salvation?

If we notice carefully the language he used, we shall see that the reference is not the same, in the two parts of his message.

The message of faith: With the heart man believeth unto righteousness, and with the mouth confession is made unto salvation; the former is the salvation that comes at once to faith—righteousness mainly in the sense of justification; the other salvation is that which is to be worked out by us in obedience and conformity to God, and, of this obedience, *confession* is the first great act. Hence also Paul says, if thou shalt confess with thy mouth Jesus *as Lord*—that is as actual ruler and sovereign of thy whole self—thou shalt be saved.

Again let us observe the *growth* of this complete salvation. Justification is instant deliverance from the *penalty* of sin; sanctification is progressive deliverance from the *power* of sin; glorification is final deliverance from the *presence* of sin.

How blessed practically to learn this holy lesson! We first repent of sin and believe on the name of the Son of God. We have thus *immediate* salvation. We are accepted in the beloved and have new standing by grace, out of the reach of all condemnation and judgment. And now, as saved saints, we are to begin a life of new and loving conformity to the will of God. We are first of all to confess Him as both Savior and Sovereign, Prophet, Priest, and King. Then we are to study conformity to His will and consecration to His service, and so grow in grace and knowledge of Himself, changed into His image from one degree of grace and glory to another; and so we shall find our salvation itself growing; we shall be saved from the dominion of sin, the sway of self, from unfruitfulness and unfaithfulness, and saved from final apostasy.

And when He comes again our blessed hope will find fruition in the perfection of a faultless as well as blameless character, and a perfect condition of heavenly bliss and glory.

Such is the salvation found in Him who is the sphere of the believer's life, the object of his justifying faith, his sanctifying love, his glorifying hope. Where else has any such salvation been found, offered, or even suggested? We hear much of the other "great religions of the world," but not one of them has even hinted the possibility of such a salvation. For that the race had to wait for a direct revelation from God out of heaven.

One thought remains to be considered: *the conditions of our entrance into this sphere of being.* How am I to get into Christ Jesus and so abide in Him? There are two sides to this matter: by *faith* as my own act, by *regeneration* as God's act. On the one hand I repent of sin, and trust in Him as my Savior. I deliberately choose to be in Him, in Him to live and move and have my being, to have Him surrounding and separating me from all else unto Himself, and providing me in Himself with all my needs and desires, and protecting me in Himself from all my fears and foes. But all this would not introduce me into Christ as the new sphere of my life, but for the power of God. It is not enough to *enter* a new sphere of life. I must have *capacity to live* in that new sphere and to breathe its atmosphere. Every form of life has its sphere, and requires adaptation to it. As we have already seen, what is life to one animal may be death to another, and reversely. If the bird is to live in the water, it needs gills; if the fish is to live in the air, it needs lungs. Every sphere of existence has its laws, and demands adaptation of nature to enter into and live in the new element. Hence He who created us must recreate us, giving us the power or right to enter this new sphere of being, and the power or capacity to receive and enjoy life in Christ Jesus. Both sides of this great matter are presented to us in one or two verses in John 1:12, 13, "As many as *received Him,* even to them that *believe on His name,* to them *gave He power* (right or authority) *to become the sons of God;* which were born not of blood, nor of the will of the flesh, nor of the will of man, but of God." Here the believing or receiving is the human act of faith, and the giving of power or capacity to become sons of God, to be born of God, is regeneration, the Divine act of new birth.

What a privilege to be thus *insphered* in Christ! Who can describe the security, the absolute safety of a disciple who abides in Him? The more we search into the wonderful Word of God, the more shall we be persuaded that there are concentric circles about God, and that the closer we get and keep to Him as center, the more immunity we shall have from evils of every sort. In the *inmost circle* of intimate fellowship perhaps no saint has ever yet dwelt. But who can limit the possibilities of a holy life? What closeness of union and communion may yet remain to be enjoyed by some who more completely than has ever yet been realized, hide themselves in the pavilion of God and abide in the secret place of the most high, under the shadow of the Almighty, covered with His breast feathers and trusting under His wings! Psalm 91.

The whole challenge of our theme is in the direction of a *full conformity to Christ.* And what is conformity, but *transformity!* Romans 12:2. To be conformed is to be transformed, to be so assimilated to God as to lose one's spiritual separation from Him.

Dr. Edward Judson calls attention to a sort of fish, or water animal, "which resembles seagrass, and hides itself in the midst of marine vegetation. Below is the head, looking like the bulb of the plant, and above is the body and the tail, looking like the blade of seagrass. The ocean currents sway the fish and the grass alike, and so the little fish escapes being devoured by its enemies. It swims along, and one can hardly perceive where fish leaves off and the grass begins, so perfect is the disguise. So a great many Christians' lives are so blended with the world that they can not easily be distinguished. They are swayed by worldly maxims and habits; they share with the world in its sinful pleasures. The difference between such Christians and worldlings is not apparent. If this is the kind of Christian life you are living, you need not be afraid of persecution; the world will not think it worth while to molest such a Christian as that. You will not know what it is to drink of the cup that Christ drank of, and to be baptized with the baptism that He was baptized with. But let a man come out into the front, let him engage in some aggressive Christian work, and he will meet the same opposition which was experienced by the One who said: 'I came not to send peace, but a sword.'"

May we not add, that it is the privilege of a disciple, on the other hand, to be so insphered in Christ as to be identified with and inseparable from Him, so that it may be a grand fact, "For to me, *to live is Christ.*" Oh, that the child of God might be so assimilated to Him that he could no longer be distinguished from Him in character and life!

What a life that would be that mortifies all that is evil and unlawful, and sanctifies all that is lawful and good.

Surely it is high time for believers to awake out of sleep! What awful apathy and lethargy exist in the matter of spiritual life and power and victory! If such final glory and triumph are assured in Christ Jesus, may not the very promise and *prospect* of such victory, the assurance of such a destiny, inspire and insure *present* holy living! These Thessalonians turned from idols to serve the living God and to wait for His Son from heaven. They served the better because they waited. Hope reacted on faith and love and obedience. No believer can truly *believe* that such final perfection of character, conquest, and reward is before him without being a stronger, better, holier man for the outlook. And the close of the first epistle is the sublime expression of this argument.

> "Abstain from every form of evil,
>   And the very God of Peace
>   Sanctify you wholly.
>   And your whole spirit, soul, and body be preserved blameless
>   Unto the coming of our Lord Jesus Christ.
>   Faithful is He that calleth you,
>   WHO ALSO WILL DO IT."
>   AMEN

VIII

General Summary of Teaching Romans to Thessalonians.

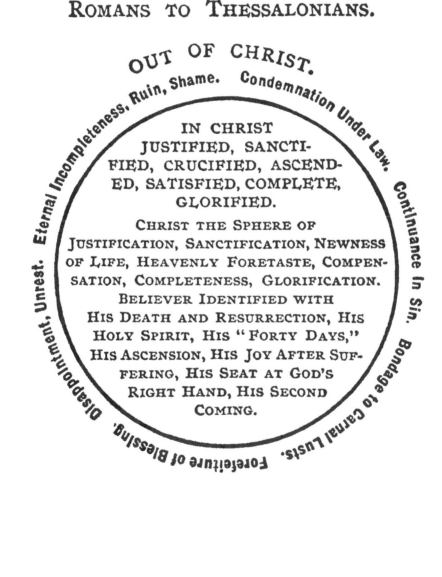

OUT OF CHRIST.

Eternal Incompleteness, Ruin, Shame.   Condemnation Under Law.

Disappointment, Unrest.

Continuance In Sin.

Bondage to Carnal Lusts.

Forfeiture of Blessing.

IN CHRIST
JUSTIFIED, SANCTI-
FIED, CRUCIFIED, ASCEND-
ED, SATISFIED, COMPLETE,
GLORIFIED.

CHRIST THE SPHERE OF
JUSTIFICATION, SANCTIFICATION, NEWNESS
OF LIFE, HEAVENLY FORETASTE, COMPEN-
SATION, COMPLETENESS, GLORIFICATION.
BELIEVER IDENTIFIED WITH
HIS DEATH AND RESURRECTION, HIS
HOLY SPIRIT, HIS "FORTY DAYS,"
HIS ASCENSION, HIS JOY AFTER SUF-
FERING, HIS SEAT AT GOD'S
RIGHT HAND, HIS SECOND
COMING.

Made in the USA
Coppell, TX
06 January 2022

71031155R00069